RELIGIONS OF THE ANCIENT EAST

IS VOLUME

141

OF THE

Twentieth Century Encyclopedia of Catholicism

UNDER SECTION

XIV

NON-CHRISTIAN BELIEFS

IT IS ALSO THE

14TH

VOLUME IN ORDER OF PUBLICATION

Edited by **HENRI DANIEL-ROPS** *of the Académie Française*

RELIGIONS OF THE ANCIENT EAST

By *ÉTIENNE DRIOTON*, *GEORGES CONTENAU* and *JACQUES DUCHESNE-GUILLEMIN*

Translated from the French by **M. B. LORAINE**

HAWTHORN BOOKS · PUBLISHERS · *New York*

© 1959 by Hawthorn Books, Inc., 70 Fifth Avenue, New York City
11. Copyright under International and Pan-American Copyright Con-
ventions. All rights reserved, including the right to reproduce this
book, or portions thereof, in any form, except for the inclusion of
brief quotations in a review. This book was manufactured in the
United States of America and published simultaneously in Canada
by McClelland & Stewart, Ltd., 25 Hollinger Road, Toronto 16. Original French edition, *Les religions de l'Orient ancien.* © Librairie
Arthème Fayard, 1957. The Library of Congress has catalogued The
Twentieth Century Encyclopedia of Catholicism under card Number
58-14327.

NIHIL OBSTAT

Joannes M. T. Barton, S.T.D., L.S.S.

Censor deputatus

IMPRIMATUR

E. Morrogh Bernard

Vicarius Generalis

Westmonasterii, die XXIX Novembris MCMLVIII

The Library of Congress has catalogued this publication as follows:

Drioton, Étienne, 1889–
    Religions of the ancient East, by Étienne Drioton, Georges
Contenau and Jacques Duchesne-Guillemin. Translated from the
French by M. B. Loraine. [1st ed.] New York, Hawthorn Books
[1959]

    164, [1] p. 21 cm. (The Twentieth century encyclopedia of Catholicism,
v. 141. Section 14: Non-Christian beliefs)

    CONTENTS.—Egyptian religion, by É. Drioton.—The ancient religions of
Western Asia, by G. Contenau.—Iranian religion, by J. Duchesne-Guillemin.—
Bibliography (p. [165])

    1. Asia, Western—Religion. 2. Egypt—Religion.   I. Title.   (Series:
The Twentieth century encyclopedia of Catholicism, v. 141)

BL1060.D713   299.2   59–6724

CONTENTS

PART I

EGYPTIAN RELIGION
by Étienne Drioton

INTRODUCTION   17

I. BELIEFS   19
   Regional Gods   19
   Gods of the Universe   19
   Secondary Gods   20
   Demi-gods or Spirits   20
   Sacred Animals   21

II. RELIGIOUS SPECULATION   22
   Mythologies   22
   Solar Mythology   23
   The Mythology of Osiris   24
   Hermopolitan Mythology   25
   Memphite Mythology   26
   Theban Mythology   26
   Theology   27
   Wisdom   28

III. THE HISTORICAL DEVELOPMENT OF EGYPTIAN
     RELIGION   31
   The Thinite Period and Old Empire   31
   The Middle Empire   32
   The Eighteenth Dynasty   33
   The Theban Theocracy   35
   The Decay of the Worship of Amon   36
   The Religion of the Late Period   36

IV. Religious Practice   38
    Temples   38
    Everyday Ritual   39
    Festivals   41
    Oracles   42
    Superstitions and Magic   42

V. Worship of the Dead   44
    Beliefs Concerning the Next World   44
        The Old Chthonian Conception   44
        Paradise   45
        The Paradise of Osiris   45
        The Solar Paradise   45
        Syncretism   46
        Judgment of the Dead   47
    Tombs   49
        Lay-out of the Tombs   49
        The Mastabas of the Old Empire   50
        The Royal Sepulchres: the Pyramids   51
        The Theban Hypogea   52
        Syncretism of the Theban Tomb   53
    Embalming and Funeral Rites   53
        Mummification   54
        Funerary Offerings   55
        Feeding Services in the Necropolis   55
        Magic Incantations   56
        Temple Endowments   57
    Conclusions   57

Part II

THE ANCIENT RELIGIONS OF WESTERN ASIA
by Georges Contenau

Introduction   63
    General Outline   63

1. Asianic Religions   66

VI. HITTITES AND HURRITES 67

 History 67
 The Pantheon 68
 Worship and Feasts 69
 Death Rites 70
 Divination and Magic 70
 Myths 71
 Images of the Gods 71
 Urartu 72
 Elam 72

VII. PHOENICIA 74

 The Gods 75
 Representations of the Gods 77
 Moral Value of the Phoenician Religion 80

 2. MESOPOTAMIA 82

VIII. SUMERIAN RELIGION 82

 Temples 86
 Sumerian Myths 87

 3. BABYLONIA AND ASSYRIA: INTRODUCTION 88

IX. HEAVEN AND THE GODS 91

 The Pantheon 91
 Myths 93
 The Character of the Gods 94

X. THE GODS AND MAN 98

 The Gods and the World 98
 The Gods and Man 100

XI. WORSHIP AND RELIGIOUS PRACTICES 105

 Worship 105
 Divination and Magic 107
 Medicine 110
 The Next World 112
 The Value of Mesopotamian Religion 113

PART III

IRANIAN RELIGION

by J. Duchesne Guillemin

INTRODUCTION   117

XII. A SHORT GLOSSARY OF IRANIAN RELIGION   120
    Iran   120
    Magians   121
    Zarathusthra   122
    Avesta   125
    Pahlavi Writings   132
    Ahura Mazda   133
    Ahriman   134
    Amasha Spantas   137
    Mithra   139
    Yima   140
    Fravarti   140
    Eschatology   143
    Saoshyant   145
    Zervanism   146
    Parseeism   149

XIII. EXTERNAL RELATIONSHIPS   151
    Iran and Greece   151
    Iran and Israel   153
    Iranian Origins and Gnosticism   161

SELECT BIBLIOGRAPHY

PART I

EGYPTIAN RELIGION
by Etienne Drioton

INTRODUCTION

Egyptian religion is like other religions of the ancient Orient in that it does not accord exactly with the modern idea of religion.

It had no sacred books containing a revelation. The Pyramid texts engraved in the tomb chambers of the last king of the fifth dynasty and of all the sixth dynasty kings, the sarcophagus texts, drawn with a calamus on the funerary urns of the Middle Empire, the Book of the Dead, copied on papyrus rolls placed near the mummies under the New Empire, cannot be regarded in this light. They were collections of magic incantations for the use of the dead in the next world. The fact that all their formulas were completely replaced by others in the course of time proves that the Egyptians reckoned none of them essential to their religion.

Furthermore, it had no final authority to define its beliefs and keep it from error. None of the functional bodies within it ever felt equipped to do this. And, apart from the radical reform of King Akh-en-Aton, whose character will be explained later, Egyptian religion had no experience of heresy. It never possessed creeds, condensing doctrine, by which the faith could be expressed in a few words. This was one result of the lack of any authority which could devise such creeds and require their use.

However, these elements, written revelation, authority and creed, are so necessary to the organization of a living religion that, when Akh-en-Aton undertook the reform of the ancient Egyptian religion, he provided it on his own accord with these three things. He made himself the infallible authority in matters of doctrine: the "teaching" which he himself gave to his followers amounted for them to revealed doctrine, only the short duration of his religion preventing it from being written down and becoming the contents of a sacred book; the name that he adopted to indicate the God of the new religion was a theological formula, containing in brief the essentials of his revelation; in other words, a true creed.

There is an easy explanation for the lack of sacred books in the traditional religion of Egypt which came before Akh-en-Aton's venture and which engulfed it after him. The origins of this religion are to be found far back in prehistoric times, when writing was unknown and oral instruction the only means of transmitting ideas. When writing was invented under the first dynasty of Pharaohs, about 3000 B.C., religious tradition was so strong and unquestionably accepted that no need was felt to write it down in definitive form and propagate it. The time for writing sacred books, necessary to every faith at the beginning, had long since passed for Egyptian religion.

Besides, the very structure of religion under the Pharaohs made impossible the constitution within it of an authority which would necessarily have exerted a unifying influence and might have given doctrine a definite shape. In fact, this religion was originally a conglomeration of local cults.

For a proper understanding of this, the peculiar way in which the Nile Valley was peopled must be examined. At first, there was no homogeneous immigration into the valley. In the paleolithic age, the whole of North Africa, covered with tropical forest, was the stamping ground of tribes of hunters, except the Nile Valley, devastated by the periodic flooding of a river more fearful than it now is and overrun by dangerous beasts. The origins of these tribes were most diverse.

During the desiccation that came with the most recent ice age, this part of the continent turned from forest into steppe and from steppe into desert. To escape the dryness, the nomad population withdrew first of all to the neighbourhood of the inland lakes, then to the Nile tributaries and finally, when these were dried up, on to the cliffs dominating the great rift through which the Nile flows; there they lived on the terraced ledges. These people, grouped in clans about a chief, in order to live had to begin by wresting from a hostile nature that part of the valley adjacent to their dwellings. When, after generations, they had achieved this, and had transferred their habitat to the centre of their new domain, the Egypt of that time emerged parcelled out into a number of minor princedoms, each independent of the rest. It is to this prehistoric period that historians, with apparent correctness, date the beginning of the worship of local gods, each sovereign in the capital of its province.

In principle, after this there was nothing to prevent a process of unification taking place in religion, like that seen in the political sphere. The obstacle to it was the manner in which the fusing together took place which, in the end, united the whole of Egypt.

The last phase is familiar. In about 3000 B.C. the only powers in a position to share the lower Nile Valley were two powerfully established, sovereign kingdoms—the southern and that of the Delta. The legendary Menes, king of the south, conquered the kingdom of the north, and, finally uniting the whole country, founded the Pharaonic monarchy. This unification, however, was brought about in a singular way: the conqueror did not force on his defeated enemy either his form of administration or his own religion; he merely took the place of his rival and assumed his traditional privileges. In religion, the king of the south simply replaced the king of the north in his rôle of son and pontiff with regard to all the gods of the Delta. It was this sonship of the king in relation to the local gods, even to those of the minor villages, which rooted the power of the Pharaohs in the country and provided the foundation of dynastic legitimacy.

This is why the Pharaonic institution, by favouring everywhere the cult of local gods, building them temples and endowing them with revenues, contributed greatly to the preservation of the most archaic traditions and to the complete upholding of an intricate polytheism, which, denied this official and ever renewed blessing, would possibly have been simplified. This is also what gives us the clear impression when we study the ancient Egyptian religion, that it was above all an amorphous collection of traditions, and that, on a final analysis, it was founded, not on a dogma to be believed, but on a cult to be practised.

CHAPTER I

BELIEFS

REGIONAL GODS

As may be understood from the foregoing, the fundamental
elements of Egyptian religion are to be found in the local gods,
each one of them lord, from time immemorial, of a part of
Egyptian territory. When the country was united politically the
gods of the most powerful cities naturally became preeminent
over the others. These unequal relationships gave rise to myths
in which the gods played new parts in accordance with their
importance.

Some of these gods were represented under forms which
varied in each case and could be animal, human or something
in between. In many cases the animal could be the god's symbol,
perhaps even its totem. The gods could therefore be shown as
completely animal, they could have an animal head on a human
body or have a completely human shape, in such a way as to
reflect a certain attribute which would recall their origin.

Local gods who were lords of their own district were not
necessarily male. A number of the primitive manors, and by
no means the lesser ones, belonged to goddesses and had done
so of old.

GODS OF THE UNIVERSE

It is not always easy to distinguish exactly between the most
ancient of the local gods, each quartered in its traditional fief,
and those others, belief in whom originated in the need to
explain the universe. The latter, known as "cosmic deities", are

due to another series of human preoccupations, in theory less ancient, but which also had its beginnings in prehistoric times. Furthermore, after the beginning of the historic period, some of the cosmic deities assumed the character of local gods, entitled to possess a temple within the district belonging especially to them. This is why, for the sake of convenience, some gods have been included in our considerations who, however, began as "cosmic". The most important were the following:

The ocean, in Egyptian Nuu, or Nun, the primordial water, origin of everything and enclosing the world on all sides.

The sky, personified in the goddess Nut, thought of as an immense woman, stretched above the earth like a vaulted arch.

The sun, in Egyptian Re, was thought to travel through the sky in two ships with their crews, the ship of night and that of the day. According to an ancient tradition he was identified with a scarab beetle, Khopri, pushing before it a ball into which it put its eggs.

The moon, usually assimilated to either Thot or Khonsu.

The stars, the most revered being Sothis, of which the helical rising, coinciding as it did with the beginning of the Nile floods, marked the new year, and Orion, which in ancient times was head of all the departed, immortalized as stars in the sky.

The earth, or Geb, husband of Nut, from whom he had been forcibly separated by Shu.

The air, personified as Shu, god of Leontopolis. This god, when time began, had slipped in between the sky and the earth who were holding on to each other in tight embrace. It had separated them by force and remained holding Nut in the air at arm's length.

SECONDARY GODS

Demi-gods or spirits

These gods, minor deities, mythopoetic inventions, or survivals from other vanished religions, were more immediately connected with the daily life of the people than were the great gods. They had no temples and played no part in the speculations of theologians.

First, there were the spirits of agriculture. Hapi, the Nile, a character suggesting fertility, dressed in a plain sailor's belt, with a bunch of papyrus reeds on top of his head; Sekhet, the fertile countryside with a lotus on the forehead; Nepri, the god of grain; Ernenutet, the goddess of the harvest, and others whose existence is only shadowy.

There was the regiment of goddesses who busied themselves with the birth of children: a frog-headed goddess, assimilated to Heket, who gave the breath of life; Meskhenet, who watched over childbirth and the seven Hathors who settled a man's destiny.

In a more general way, Thueris, while affording special protection to pregnant women, was a powerful defence against evil spirits, with her heavy hippopotamus's body, crocodile's jaws, lioness's feet and woman's hands. The deformed and merry dwarf, Bes, with hairy beard and dangling tongue, distended belly and twisted legs and leopard's tail, performed the same duties and also looked after music, dancing and personal toilet.

Sacred animals

The worship of living animals, thought of as incarnations of gods enjoying the adoration of believers, was one of the peculiarities of Egyptian religion which made a striking impression on Greek travellers when they first began to visit and describe Egypt.

The best known of such animals were these: the bulls Apis, incarnation of Ptah at Memphis, Mnevis of the sun at Heliopolis, and Bukis of Montu at Hermonthis; the ram of Amon at Thebes, of Khnum at Elephantine and that of Harsaphes at Heracleopolis; the goat of Osiris at Busiris and Menides; the crocodile of Sebek at Fayum and the cat of Bastet at Bubastis.

CHAPTER II

RELIGIOUS SPECULATION

MYTHOLOGIES

These numerous divine individual beings could not exist together in Egyptian religion without relations being established between them. In fact, none of these territorial gods continued as the "only, solitary god" as they probably were when at the head of the tribes still wandering in the deserts bordering on Egypt during the aeneolithic age. By settling, together with their worshippers, in the Nile Valley, these gods were established as powerful territorial lords, each in what amounted to his palace: that is, the main temple of the capital from which his son would rule, the kinglet of the *nomos*. There each acquired children in order to suit the clan alliances made necessary by political conditions. In this way local "trios" sprung up, which would appear to be the earliest attempts made to establish a divine hierarchy, following the degree of importance of the still independent cities.

The combination of these various cults did not come about without the formation of mythical legends about the gods in question whereby their stories were traced back and the worship they received justified. Very little remains of these primitive myths in the hieroglyphic texts, in which the god of each city acted as the supreme god. The local trios were swept up, recast and absorbed in the even vaster synthetic developments which claimed to provide each of those little pre-dynastic kingdoms with a religious system adequate for its territorial power, and guaranteeing the supremacy of each god in its capital, while simultaneously the uniting of the whole of Egypt was in progress. In this way the great theological syntheses came into being which, though irreconcilable in spite of the efforts of later theologians, were perpetuated in Egyptian religion right up to the end. The final unification of Egypt under Menes should have caused Egyptian religion to be recast and unified as well. An attempt to do this was actually made under the first dynasties, by the priesthood of Memphis, as is mentioned later; but belief in this does not seem to have extended beyond the borders or the *nomos* of Memphis. Religious beliefs had become too complicated in the prehistoric period and they so persisted under cover of an artificial unity which neither Memphite mythology nor the later mythology of Amon of Thebes could manage to transform into a real unity.

The syntheses which, by their compound character, rather than by a proper blending, formed the foundation of Egyptian religion were the following: the solar and Osirian mythologies, both of them dating from the prehistoric age, during which they came together in peaceful contact after a period of violent antagonism; that of Thot, the remains of a short-lived dominance of the town of Hermopolis over Middle Egypt during the same period; then the mythology of Memphis, elaborated during the historic period, going back to the first dynasties, and that of Thebes, which appeared in the Middle Empire.

Solar mythology

Evolved at Heliopolis, this mythology regarded the sun as the supreme deity; according to this, at the beginning of time there was nothing but the primordial water, motionless, dark and cold, Nun or Chaos. First of all the sun, Atum, had created himself therein. Then, by spitting, according to some, or masturbating, according to others, he had produced the first couple, Shu and Tefnut who had given birth to Geb, the earth god, and Nut, the sky goddess. After Shu had separated the sky from the earth, lifting Nut above his head while her mate remained prostrate, Nut gave birth, one after the other, to Osiris, Seth, Isis and Nephtys, the protagonists of Osirian legend. This group of nine deities made up the greater Ennead. The lesser

Ennead, with Horus as head, contained gods of secondary importance.

Built around these speculative notions, the solar mythology had also its true legends, full of poetry, freshness and sometimes of humour. There was the story, for instance, of how, when time began, a lotus bud, sunk deep in chaos, had opened its corolla above the waters and let out the sun in the shape of a delicate child. Some texts state that the sun had wept and that the tears congealed into men when they touched the earth.

The mythology of Osiris

The wondrous tales about Osiris and the gods of his cycle are not so much mythology as legend, as they give no indication of attention paid to cosmogony, the main theme of Egyptian mythologies. They appear to be of popular origin, a fact which would explain their preservation, in spite of being embodied very early into official mythology, of such a dramatic character and the constant preference shown to them by the great mass of people. The legend of Osiris, references to which may be found in Egyptian texts from the earliest period onwards, is set out in full in Greek, in Plutarch's work, "On Isis and Osiris", written at the end of the first century A.D. in accordance with ancient traditions.

Osiris was the oldest son of Geb, the earth god, and Nut, the sky goddess, and thereby heir to the kingdom of the world. Once in possession of his inheritance he ruled it as a beneficent monarch. But his brother, Seth, the Typhon of the Greek version, having been excluded from power, grew jealous and began to plot against his authority. According to the old texts, Seth succeeded in capturing Osiris, killing him and throwing his corpse into the water, no details being given of the actual murder.

It is otherwise in the Greek version of the story. In this, while admittedly it may use the material of an ancient tradition, Typhon made a feast for Osiris at which the guests were his accomplices. During the meal he had a splendidly wrought chest brought in of which the length corresponded intentionally with Osiris' unusual height, and declared jokingly that he would give it as a present to whomsoever should fit it exactly by lying in it. Several of the guests tried unsuccessfully but, as soon as Osiris, suspecting nothing, had lain down in it, the conspirators slammed the lid, nailed the chest shut and then threw it into the Nile, which bore it towards the sea.

The oldest form of the legend has it that Isis and Nephtys had set out to look for the corpse of Osiris and found it still in Egypt, covered with mud and already decomposing. According to the Pyramid texts, Geb had cleaned off the mud and Nut had re-set the limbs, Re had bidden him awake, at which Osiris had revived. A Middle Empire source introduces the custom of mummification, by this time universal, and has it that Re had sent Anubis the embalmer from heaven to see to the body of Osiris. In the words of a hymn in the Louvre, Isis then beat the air with his wings above the mummy, Osiris started to breathe and sat up, restored to life.

None of these ancient sources represents Osiris as having taken over again his earthly kingdom which, after many vicissitudes, fell to his son, Horus the Child, who overthrew Seth and avenged his father. Death had ended the reign of Osiris, and even when restored to life, it was only in the other world that he was king thereafter.

Hermopolitan mythology

At Hermopolis, the supreme local god, Thot, the moon god, ibis or baboon, was the originator of all things. He himself had awoken in the depths of chaos, then, with his voice, summoned into existence the Ogdoad, or group of eight gods whose business it was to prepare for the birth of the sun. This Ogdoad consisted of eight couples, the males having frogs' heads and the females those of snakes. Their names, in both masculine and feminine forms were, Night, Darkness, Mystery and Eternity. A faint outline can here be detected of later gnostic speculations on the Aeons. The Ogdoad had established itself on a mound which emerges from the void at Hermopolis itself and there produced the egg from which the sun made its appearance. The latter first overcame all adverse powers and then created and organized the world.

Memphite mythology

At other centres of worship cosmogonies were invented to the advantage of the local god, based largely on those of Heliopolis or Hermopolis, sometimes mingling elements of both.

Thus, at Memphis, Ptah was raised to the highest rank in the Egyptian Pantheon when the town was founded as the capital of the new, united kingdom, at the beginning of the first dynasty. Ptah then assumed the theological title of "Ta tenen" or "Earth that emerged", as being a personification of the first mound, this being borrowed from Hermopolis. In creating himself he had thereby given existence also to eight other Ptahs, as parts of himself. These became the great gods of Egypt and made up, with the first Ptah, the Egyptian Ennead, as at Heliopolis. The members of this Ennead were only hypostases of Ptah: for instance Atum was his thought, Horus his heart, Thot his tongue. The world had been created through his voice, as at Hermopolis.

Theban mythology

In the same way, when the local god of Karnak, Amon Re, became the god of an empire, he also became head of an Ennead, modelled in some ways on that of Heliopolis, otherwise formed by the addition of Amon to the eight gods of Hermopolis. Along with the system of divine origins, the cosmogonic ideas of Heliopolis and Hermopolis joined together, the proportions of the mixture varying to suit the taste of individual theorists, and became the mythology of Amon Re. So, according to the mythological texts carved by Ptolemy VIII on the second pylon at Karnak, it was taught at this time in Thebes, making use of old manuscripts in the language of the New Empire, that, in the beginning, Amon lay still under the waters of Nun until, taking a foothold on the foundation that was to become Thebes, he awoke. He drew forth this land, dried it thoroughly with his own heat and made it the first mound on which he created the Eight. Only then did he reveal himself as the sun.

THEOLOGY

There was a rudimentary theology in the syntheses that we have sketched out. These were not entirely made up of mythical tales but, through the interpretation of the images of myth, sought to express thoughts, and even theories, concerning the divine order.

The legend of Osiris has one peculiar feature. It was above all a myth with moral meaning suggesting and commending to men of all degree the justice and beneficence of Osiris, the conjugal fidelity of Isis, the pains taken by Horus to re-establish his father and avenge his memory. In the final defeat of Seth and his friends, it offered a solution to the problem of evil. Only slight speculation is contained in this legend. It was also possible, as in fact was done, to insert any other dogmatic synthesis into the framework of the myth without upsetting it.

It was not so with the other syntheses. All of them admitted and applied in their own way the principle of henotheism according to which one god more powerful than the rest was placed at the head of these, a god *par excellence*, *neter neten*, or "divine god" in the theological terminology of Egypt. Memphite theology went beyond the Heliopolitan and definitely made the lesser gods the mere hypostases of Ptah. In this it came close to monotheism.

The creation processes set in motion by the supreme god went back to two principles; in Heliopolitan theology the first created beings, the divine couple Shu and Tefnut, had been physically given out from the sun's own flesh; Hermopolitan theology had invented the subtler method of creation by the voice, and this idea was to flourish in later speculations, especially those of Memphis.

It must not be thought, however, that solar theology was inferior in ingenuity to Hermopolitan ideas. In order to soften the crudity of the oldest myths of creation, Heliopolis invented the notion of Maet, goddess of justice, daughter of Re and immanent in him, through whom the sun had created and then ruled all things. This notion was also destined to become popular; it is found later in the *khokma* of the Hebrew books of wisdom and in the Logos of the Platonist Jew Philo.

WISDOM

Finally, there is an imposing series of texts which have not normally been taken into consideration by historians of Egyptian religion, as they are not, properly speaking, religious works. Nevertheless, these writings are imbued with the spirit of religion, like the whole of the civilization of ancient Egypt, and may therefore bring light to bear upon the religious ideas of the most educated classes.

Sapiential literature was very fashionable in Ancient Egypt. For each period the most highly regarded works have come down to us, whole or in part. These books were manuals of living, in the highest sense of the expression. They aimed at forming subjects able to lead good lives, that is, to think rightly and behave honestly at court and in society. They were taught in the schools and show, in works ranging from the Old Empire to the Greco-Roman period, a consistent and continuous tradition. For hundreds, even thousands, of years, under literary forms differing slightly with the taste of the time, there runs a dominant spirit which is none other than the general opinion of thinking people, one of the bases of the old Egyptian civilization.

The deity is frequently invoked in these sapiential writings; in a form, moreover, surprising at first sight for Ancient Egypt, as it appears, quite simply, as God, as in monotheistic religions. Below are some quotations by way of documentary illustration; one example is taken from among many others like it, from each of the old Egyptian books of wisdom which have come down to us:

Instruction to Kagemmi (*c.* 2700 B.C.) Pap. Prisse, 2, 2.
"Beware of being relentless:

no man knows what God can cause to happen when he punishes."

Instructions of Ptah Hotep (*c.* 2450 B.C.) Pap. Prisse, 6, 8.

"Do not give cause for fear among men, for God chastises the same way."

Instruction to Merikare (*c.* 2070 B.C.), lines 49–50.

"God knows the unjust man,
God chastises his faults even unto blood."

Wisdom of Anu (*c.* 1450 B.C.), maxim 35.

"Let him who accuses thee give his reasons, following God's example, who discerns the upright."

Wisdom of Amenemope (*c.* 750 B.C.?), 8, 19–20.

"A bushel given thee by God is better than five thousand wrongly gained."

Inscriptions of Petosiris (*c.* 300 B.C.), 137.

"To one kindly of heart, God is kindly."

Expressions of this sort, which occur uninterruptedly throughout Egyptian literature, are not only to be found in sapiential writings. It could be put forward, as has been done, that it is only a kind of universal set expression which, in the books used by the young scribes who had come from different provinces to schools at the royal court, took the place of the name of each one's local god. However, the same phrase is often found in ordinary language, in which case the above explanation is valueless. "I have pleased God because he loved me, remembering that I should reach God the day of my death", said the monarch Hapijefa about 1950 B.C. in the inscription on his tomb at Assiut. "I was truly a good man, free of fault, putting God in his heart and acknowledging his power", proclaimed Beki, the titular of a stele in the Museum of Turin dating from about 1450 B.C. This is echoed in many inscriptions carved as pious mottoes on the scarabs of this same period: "The favoured of God is he who loves him", "God loves the one who loves him", "God exalts him who loves him", "God is the protector of my life", "Life belongs to the favoured of God", "Nourishing me is God's duty", and so on.

So imposing a collection of texts is enough to convince one that there existed a monotheistic stream, or at least a way of expressing things, in the religious thought of Ancient Egypt, and that from the Old Empire onwards, or practically since the beginning of Pharaonic civilization. On the other hand, it is no less certain that monotheism never crystallized into a cult, except perhaps during the reform of Akh-en-Aton of which more will be said.

CHAPTER III

THE HISTORICAL DEVELOP-MENT OF EGYPTIAN RELIGION

As with the history of the Pharaonic period as a whole, so it is with its religious history: what little we know is from the inscriptions, which are of the nature of official statements in which everything is described as going quite smoothly. Only far-reaching revolutions or serious turmoil left any traces and that indirectly.

THE THINITE PERIOD AND OLD EMPIRE

We have only a few pieces of evidence in the old religious writings known as the Pyramid Texts for the religious struggles which raged during the prehistoric period in the efforts made to ensure for this god or that the obedience of one or other of the districts. Just before the unification of Egypt by Menes, about 3000 B.C., the south and north worshipped the same gods, which had the same legends, and the two conflicting royal families both claimed descent from the same mythical ancestor, the God Horus.

The dynastic religion of united Egypt continued, therefore, to be that of Horus. Nevertheless, it is possible to gather from certain indications that the history of this religion was not so peaceful as might be believed and that it was disturbed by the conflicting streams deriving from old, individualistic traditions which would not die.

Coming to the fifth dynasty, which began about 2560 B.C., we encounter something new, fraught with consequence, for it set Egyptian religion on the path it was to follow up to the end of the Pharaonic civilization, namely the adoption of the Heliopolitan belief as the official doctrine of the monarchy. The latter's dynastic god, Horus the Falcon, was then identified with the supreme god of the Ennead of Heliopolis, Atum, known by his name of Harakhtes, and the kings proclaimed themselves definitely sons of Re. Wherever possible, solar mythology absorbed local mythologies. Their gods had to become so many hypostases of Re: Khnum-Re, Montu-Re, Sebek-Re, even Atum-Re, purely formally, as he was already the sun. Only Ptah and Thot, because they were gods with too powerful followings of priests, and Osiris, because his over popular legend could not be readapted, remained untouched by any assimilation to Re.

THE MIDDLE EMPIRE

At the end of the sixth dynasty, about 2300 B.C., there occurred a phenomenon in funerary religion, to which a later chapter will be dedicated, which modern historians have called democratization: it was accompanied by the increasing popularity among all classes of society of the cult of Osiris.

Under the eleventh dynasty, an important political event gave this moment of popular piety definite official consecration. King Antef II (2120–2070 B.C.), while engaged in his struggle with the kings of Heracleopolis, captured Abydos, where the necropolis contained the cenotaphs of the old Thinite kings. In order to harness the influence of devotion to Osiris to the furthering of his own cause, the king established Osiris there, along with Khentamentiu. The latter was soon assimilated to the former. From this time onwards Osiris became and remained definitely the great God of the dead.

In a different sphere, that of god of the living, the accession of the twelfth dynasty about 2000 B.C. opened up an age of renewed supremacy for a new form of Heliopolitan doctrine, transplanted into Theban soil to the worship of Amon, god of Karnak, originally too lowly to avoid becoming Amon-Re. Under this name the god took his place at the head of the pantheon.

THE EIGHTEENTH DYNASTY

The rise to power of Amon-Re

Under the Hyksos domination the prestige of the god of the royal dynasty was added to by his continuing to be the national god; during the war of independence waged by the Theban princes of the seventeenth dynasty, by his becoming the god of liberation, and, in the period of the Asiatic conquests of the eighteenth dynasty, by his being the god who subdued foreign nations and left them to the mercy of his sons, the Pharaohs. In this way political events turned Amon into a god whose power was everywhere recognized as all high and universal. He, and his priesthood with him, enjoyed a revenue unheard of before that time which confirmed and consolidated this power: namely a certain share of the treasure captured from the enemy, of the temples of conquered countries and their funds, of trains of prisoners sent for forced labour, not to omit the buildings constructed around the Temple of Karnak, as befitted a royal piety, which in a very short time made this temple a magnificently fabulous architectural group.

The religious reform of Akh-en-Aton

This abundance of riches, no less than the excessive influence which it gave to the priests, brought about the downfall of Amon.

Already, near the end of his reign, Amenophis III (1408–1372 B.C.), uneasy about the growing power of the priests of Amon, had grown cooler towards the great god of Karnak. He had removed his palace to the left bank of the Nile, at some distance from the temple and there, in a private chapel, he favoured a sun worship which was supposed to revert to the pure Heliopolitan tradition without reference to Amon. His son, Amenophis IV (1372–1354 B.C.) shared these ideas and made no secret of it. So, in the fourth year of his reign, at the first sign of difficulty with the Theban priesthood, he precipitated the crisis that loomed over him.

The inscriptions of the period enable us to define his position regarding doctrine. He returned to the Heliopolitan cult of Re-Harakhtes, considering Amon as a usurper of the divine throne. The usual punishment accorded to intruders was applied to him: his name was proscribed together with the names of the gods of his family and of the gods under him, in short, of all the gods. But since in popular belief and according to the most basic dictate of Egyptian religion Amon remained liege-lord spirit of Karnak, even when stripped of supreme power and blackened in reputation, Amenophis IV left Theban territory and founded somewhat upstream of Hermopolis and on the other bank, on land intact from any previous divine overlordship, a new capital, which he dedicated to the god of his purified religion.

The religion of Heliopolis was never popular in character, at any rate since the historic period. Amenophis undertook to make it so. He chose the solar Disk as the visible manifestation of Harakhtes, following tradition, but he characterized it as the symbol of his reform by showing it as a sun of which the rays ended in hands pointing towards the earth, ready for action anywhere at any time.

For, according to the new doctrine, Aton, the Disk, acted in everything without intermediary, as he had done in the beginning for the creation. Once at this stage, the personal doctrine of Amenophis IV was formally monotheistic and it was in this form that he tried to impose it. Egypt and the provinces were, by royal edict, to have no more than one god, Aton. The king changed his own name, which contained that of Amon, to Akh-en-Aton, the servant of Aton. He named his capital Akhet-Aton, the Horizon of Aton.

Akh-en-Aton had not invented a monotheism non-existent

in Egypt before him but he desired to make it the foundation of a new worship, purified of all error. In this he was faithful to his notion of establishing what he called Truth in all fields (we should call it logic) and he resolved to put an end to the contradiction always felt by enlightened minds between the philosophical monotheism professed by the educated classes and their actual polytheism. Coming straight to the heart of the matter, he chose one of the two parallel traditions and rejected the other. His originality lies in the firmness of his choice and the daring of his denial.

But in doing this he committed, properly speaking, a heresy, in its primary etymological sense, since he was attacking one order of truths as uncontradictable in the eyes of his contemporaries as the other, for it had reached them in the same way, the sacrosanct way of immemorial tradition. His aggressive monotheism, which recked nothing of all the old territorial overlordships, the foundation of religion, was too opposed to Egyptian thought to be able to be understood. So, as soon as Akh-en-Aton had died, in the reign of Tutankhamen, Egypt returned enthusiastically to Amon and its traditional gods. There was no more of Akh-en-Aton for several years except to curse him, destroy his monuments and proscribe his name, as he had done for Amon. Then his memory sank into the deepest oblivion.

THE THEBAN THEOCRACY

With this storm over, Amon and his priests were restored to all their privileges. Then, in the peaceful but somnolent Egypt of the last Rameses (1166–1105 B.C.), we find a gradual movement, in consequence of all the weakening of royal power, towards the theocracy foreseen and aspired to by Akh-en-Aton. This movement, and afterwards the political success of this system with the priest kings (1105–950 B.C.), reshaped the character of the religion of Amon. Amon began to concern himself more directly and more often in human affairs. Confronted with the inefficacy of the royal judges, he began to cut short the everyday cases of his faithful with oracles. When the king failed to concede funerary privileges he supplied decrees in their favour, addressed to the gods of the other world.

Towards the end of the twentieth dynasty, the old Egyptian religion received another jolt: the War of the Unclean, which M. Pierre Montet has recently brought to light in recognizing the historical value of a passage from the historian Manethou, before believed to be nothing more than legendary. The worshippers of Seth, who had kept themselves in large numbers around Avarais, the old capital of the Hykros kings, clashed with the Pharaohs of Thebes and terrorized Egypt for thirteen years. In the end, the high priest Amenophis, in the reign of Rameses IX (*c.* 1090 B.C.), cut them to pieces and expelled the remainder to Asia.

THE DECAY OF THE WORSHIP OF AMON

The capture and sack of Thebes by Asshurbanipal in 663 B.C., and its definite abandonment as the capital, delivered the fatal blow to the worship of Amon. He began to be an abstract deity, a theological entity. Popular devotion came to centre round the goddesses of the successive capitals, Bastis of Bubastis and Neith of Sais. Later, following on the repeated defeats of the national kings, and under the two Persian dominations (524–404 and 341–330 B.C.), it preferred gods of flesh and bone, the sacred animals, who had not abandoned the people throughout all the misfortunes of the nation. Faith in the old gods concentrated on them and, in the end, worshippers of one sacred animal adored the whole species.

THE RELIGION OF THE LATE PERIOD

In this sketch of the development of Egyptian religion the emphasis has been on the history of solar worship, the most important of Ancient Egypt, as, for twenty centuries, it was the official cult of the Pharaonic monarchy.

Beside it, the most important cult was that of Osiris, god of the dead and the favourite in popular devotion. After violent rivalry in the prehistoric period, and its recurrence at the beginning of the fifth dynasty concerning the posthumous fate of the kings, this worship of Osiris existed peacefully with worship of the Sun in the religion of the Egyptians. Any weakening of the solar dogma was bound to strengthen it, sun religion being tied to the vicissitudes of the national monarchy. When this was overwhelmed in the turmoil of the Persian invasion in 525 B.C. faith in Osiris, which bore the explanation of all evils and allowed any sort of hope, remained intact. It was even so flourishing that the first Greek travellers took it to be the expression of the national religion of Egypt.

The Hellenism which took root in Egypt through the conquest of Alexander and which developed quickly began to undermine the old religion of the Egyptians in turning them away from their ancestral traditions. In vain did the Ptolemies, successors of Alexander, attempt to give their subjects, Egyptians and Hellenes alike, a common worship, that of Serapis. The old religion was on its last legs under Roman domination at which time it began to be overwhelmed by the irresistible rise of Christianity.

CHAPTER IV

RELIGIOUS PRACTICE

TEMPLES

Egyptian worship was conducted in consecrated buildings, to the development and decoration of which the reigning sovereigns always devoted the utmost care and also great riches. They did this out of filial piety to the local gods, whose descendants and heirs they claimed to be, so as to be granted prosperity for themselves and their kingdoms by these deities.

The Egyptian temple had this peculiarity; it was not a place of sacrifice at the disposal of the people, like the temples of Semitic cults; it was still less a place for religious meetings or sermons like the synagogue and afterwards of the church and the mosque. It was a private residence, the personal palace of a god. This strongly marked characteristic governed the architectural lay-out and the forms of worship practised within it.

In the first place, the Egyptian temple was not open to all comers. Its buildings were quite enclosed by a thick wall of rough brick, in every way like a fortress. Entry could only be effected through fortified gates, or pylons. Just as the villa of a great lord was put up in the centre of all his holdings, the sacred enclosure included gardens with a sacred lake, workshops and warehouses, lodgings for priests and workmen, all outside the actual temple. This was built of stone, the eternal material, whereas the rest was only built of rough brick. Its plan, even when realized in gigantic proportions, was extremely simple. Through the pylons, on the same level, was a court surrounded by porches; at the other end was an inclined plane leading to a gallery of pillars or columns, built on a stylobate and extending to the whole width of the court. A door in the middle of this gallery led to the sanctuary, where the idol of the cult was shut up in a tabernacle or *naos*. The sanctuary was narrow and dark and did not extend to the width of the temple as the other chambers had done. Sometimes chapels of deities associated with the cult of the principal god were built on other sides; or else, as under the Ptolemies, the main sanctuary was surrounded by a ring of chambers and separated from them by a curved passage.

This simple plan, an adaptation of the basic features of the Egyptian lordly mansion, pleasure ground, reception room and private apartments, was the same in all Egyptian temples. In spite of a few variations, it is easily recognizable in the best preserved and therefore most famous temples—Luxor, Dair el Bahari, Abydos, the Rameseum, Abu Simbal, Madinat Habu, from the New Empire, and Philae, Edful, Kom Ombo and Denderah, dating from the Greco-Roman period. The apparent complication in the group of buildings at Karnak is due to the massing together in a comparatively restricted space of a number of temples of this kind, each one being in itself quite straightforward. The complication is added to by the fact that the kings of the eighteenth dynasty signalled their devotion to Amon by building courts and pylons one after another before the original sanctuary. They are now in ruins but numbered ten altogether.

EVERYDAY RITUAL

In temples regarded as lordly manors, the worship itself assumed as a consequence a special quality. Just as a mighty Egyptian would not open his dwelling to be invaded by the mob, so the god reserved entry into his temple to his own intimates; service was to be carried out as quietly and discreetly as possible. Worship, in so far as it concerned direct relationships with the god, was performed by a restricted group of servants. In theory, the king, as the son of each god, was his only high priest: hence, in the religious scenes carved on the walls of the temples, it is always he who is represented as celebrating. In fact, sacred ceremonies were performed by priests acting in his stead, divided into tribes which took turns by the month for the performance of worship. The major officials were important civil servants, who usually had several priestly positions. Minor officials were the permanent servers of the temple.

Ceremonies began early in the morning, but, even when the sun was high, the sanctuary, being without any opening, was still in darkness. The duty priest lit the lamps, prepared the censer and made a preliminary censing to spread a pleasant odour in the room.

Then he would go towards the *naos*. He would break the seal set on the bolt of the doors by his colleague of the day before at the end of the last service. He opened the leaves of the doors. There was the idol, but, according to belief, still inert and asleep, for the godhead had not yet come down into it. The priest would prostrate himself and recite a hymn of adoration. Then, getting up, he embraced the statue. This, being the action of a son who would wake his father from sleep, "awoke" the god and brought his divine spirit down into him. True worship could now begin.

The priest would then perform the god's toilet. He washed the idol; he decked it with clothing and jewellery brought by the robe keepers, then he perfumed it and applied cosmetics. After this he offered the god his morning meal by consecrating to him an offering of bread, meat, vegetables, fruit and various drinks, laid out on a tray placed on a little table, as in the manors of the nobility. For this purpose he held a war club over the food and drink, a symbolic action whereby he sacrificed them mystically and sent their spirit into the invisible world, the world of the gods. This is perhaps the sole vestige of the very old conception of sacrifice in Egyptian liturgy, analogous to that of the Semites who consecrated victims to the gods by sacrificing them. After this action, the remains left on the altar were removed to provide for the servants of the temple and those privileged persons to whom the king had made grants of food from the sacred revenues.

The statue of the god was then undressed and once more purified and perfumed. The priest shut the doors of the *naos*, which he sealed with his seal. Then he withdrew backwards, wiping out as he went the marks of his feet from the fine sand spread out over the flag stones.

Such was the ceremony for the first meal. It was repeated several times a day, not only for the chief god, but for all the various idols which had chapels around the temple sanctuary.

The people took no part in the ceremonies performed in the temple. At the most, the first court would be opened to them on certain feast days. The rest of the time they had to be satisfied with adoring the sculpted images outside the temples, and the gods in the prayer-houses of confraternities which were very numerous in the towns, or even in the domestic shrines found in private houses.

FESTIVALS

It was in festal celebrations that popular devotion reached the highest splendour. When the king wished to show himself to his people he would come out of the palace and pass through the streets of the town with great ceremony, and then hold court in some place prepared specially for the event. The gods of Egypt behaved in the same way. On feast days, their statues were carried in procession out of the temples and the priests exposed them on the way in chapels of repose for the adoration of the faithful. The Greeks, struck by the large numbers of people who flocked to them, called them "panegyries" (solemn assemblies of all the people).

An Egyptian town celebrated the important events in the earthly life of their god in this way, especially his birth and victory over his enemies. They also celebrated the New Year, the beginning of every month, the Nile Flood and the beginning of the harvest. Several times a year, the statue of the god was embarked on the river to visit the neighbouring deities and take part in their feasts. On every occasion the idol was brought out in a procession and exposed in several places to the adoration of the faithful. There was also everywhere one festival more solemn than the rest, a "Great Outing" which took on the appearance of a patronal feast: for this the statue was paraded through the town and its outskirts for several days, and was lodged every evening in a prayer-house that lay on its route. At these times great nocturnal rejoicing resounded throughout the illuminated cities.

ORACLES

Oracles came to occupy an increasingly important position in the religious life of the Egyptians. The most authentic were those given out by the statue of the god itself, when it came out in procession. Important decisions were left to it, and it would answer "yes" or "no" by means of the forward or backward movements which it supposedly made its porters perform. At other times, two sheets of papyrus on which the contradictory proposals had been written would be presented to the god and it would point out the correct one by moving towards it. A number of questions were decided in this way, especially cases of theft and detection of robbers.

The presence of idols in the minor sanctuaries of the town and country encouraged the frequent consulting of oracles of this sort. The gods most questioned at Thebes were Khonsu, and also king Amenophis I and Queen Nefertari, who had been deified in the necropolis.

One of the reasons for the popularity of sacred animals in the last period is undoubtedly to be found in the fashion prevailing for their oracles. They were easy to consult. Apis the bull, when set loose in his enclosure, gave a favourable answer or not, according to whether he turned right or left. The sacred bull of Medamud granted or refused his approval by coming or holding back when the inquirer called.

SUPERSTITIONS AND MAGIC

The picture here presented of Egyptian religion would be

incomplete, or run the risk of being distorted, if no mention were made of the position of superstition and magic.

The observance of propitious and unpropitious days, worked out from tables referring to mythical happenings, and the interpretation of dreams, greatly preoccupied the Egyptians.

It is remarkable that magic had no place in the official worship conducted in the temples; on the other hand, it was the basis of all funeral rites and worship of the dead. In ordinary life it was thought to be a science whereby protection was obtained from all evil spirits and dangers of any sort. It acted through recited formulas and especially amulets, which were widely used in all classes of society.

CHAPTER V

WORSHIP OF THE DEAD

BELIEFS CONCERNING THE NEXT WORLD

If any conviction was firmly anchored in the minds of the ancient Egyptians, it was that man survived after death. The conception they had formed of how man was made up is still not quite clearly understood. Besides the body, they attributed two elements to man, more or less ghostly and independent of matter: the "ba" which can apparently be rendered exactly by "soul" and which they used to represent as a bird with human head; and the "ka" in which some Egyptologists have seen an immaterial reflection of man's body, a "double", whereas others, more recently, have viewed it as a protective spirit that is born with the man and looks after him after his death.

Whatever the truth may be, death was definitely regarded by the Egyptians as being the separation of the spiritual and corporal elements of man.

The old chthonian conception

The first element in their belief, and presumably the most ancient, was that the immaterial principle of man, his spirit, continued to live in close connection with the corpse and even depending on it.

The tomb in which the corpse was buried gave access, through its funerary pit, to a region barred to the living. The cell into which the body was lowered became the eternal dwelling place of the soul. The latter, in its underworld existence, found refuge and rest in it and was there fed by the worship offered by the living. The life it led below was undoubtedly somewhat diminished but, if all necessary measures were taken, it could be quite peaceful and even happy.

Paradise

Understandably, the different cults, evidence of which is to be found in the ancient monuments, opened up to their believers visions of posthumous existence more attractive than the underground existence just mentioned. As was natural, these cults promised their faithful great happiness in the company of the gods they had served upon earth.

The paradise of Osiris

The kingdom of Osiris was "the West", an extra-territorial region personified as the goddess who welcomed the dead, the lovely Amentet. The god, having acquired blessed immortality thanks to the burial rights performed for him by Anubis, reigned over this place which was later to be identified, when the geography of the other world had been harmonized, with the Field of Offerings and the Field of Yam, the Elysian Fields of the Greeks.

This was the paradise reserved by Osiris for his believers, that is to those of them who, having enjoyed the same rites as he, have become Osirians and therefore his subjects for all eternity.

The solar paradise

Belief in a paradise of the Sun was born and developed well after the historic period had begun.

In its oldest state, it does not seem that solar religion possessed any particular eschatology: it governed men during their lives and then left them after death to the care of the chthonian gods in their underworld domains.

It was at the beginning of the fifth dynasty, about 2560 B.C., with the accession of a royal family from Heliopolis which held its beliefs, that believers in solar doctrine began to work out a place for the dead in the framework of their theology. It was done at first for the benefit of the king, to whom they assured a fate different from that of ordinary mortals. Special ablutions, a kind of baptism of the dead, conferred the dignity of Heliopolitan on the dead being, and opened the door of the Empyreum to him. He was then admitted into the Sun's own boats. In order to achieve unsullied happiness, the beings of the Old Empire included their wives, children and other members of the family in this plan. The ablutions were accorded to them also and, with this, the right to solar immortality.

It followed perhaps for political reasons and because the impoverished monarchy of the sixth dynasty could otherwise no longer be sure of their fidelity, that the kings extended this privilege to their courtiers and officials.

It is not difficult to understand the popularity of this notion towards the end of the Old Empire of sharing the royal fate, in a country like Egypt, for ever a land of officials; the sharing being regarded as a mark of favour in this world and a guarantee of bliss in the next. A nobility of eternity was thus created. Afterwards, there was no minor provincial official who did not aspire to this favour, nor Egyptian who did not covet it. The literature of the end of the Memphite period is full of the recriminations of the old aristocrats against this rush to obtain funeral privileges and the ease with which they were obtained from the king.

So it was, that, as the royal power crumbled at the end of the Old Empire and there came about the so-called democratization of privileges of all degrees formerly reserved for the court, and the privilege of sharing in the royal fate underwent the same process. Anyone in Egypt who could exercise the slightest authority was permitted to set up a tomb at his own expense, with all the traditional circumstance of the great privileged class of the time of the Pyramids. Automatically, solar destiny became common property.

Syncretism

The Egyptians always exhibited extraordinary restraint in making use of the different paradises at their disposal. This is explained by the fact that in the end they found it impossible to give up their old tomb ideology. The very layout of the sepulchres they built and the rites they celebrated proclaimed too loudly that souls remained in the tomb. Perhaps, too, their taste for the life of this world dissuaded them from abandoning completely, for the sake of a remote paradise, the tomb they had prepared at great expense during their life and which they had endowed with all that was necessary for their external comfort. Furthermore, belief in paradises of the various gods never became part of the teaching concerning the fate of souls except as a possibility of escape from the tomb, and everybody was free to take it or leave it.

By borrowing from each theological system such advantages as he could, the Egyptian finally worked out a mean programme for his life after death. He would spend the daytime in the cool air of his cell, using the provisions brought to him by his descendants or found for him by magic; at nightfall, he would join the Sun's boat and stop it, to board, and then to cross the horizon and pass safely through the inaccessible and dangerous regions of the other side; he could, if he wished, get out in the fields of Osiris, or any other paradise in which he could amuse himself agreeably. As soon as the Sun was ready to leave this fabulous country, which was itself to be plunged into darkness, he would rejoin the ship of Re, cross the eastern horizon in it and be reborn with it into this world; he would then hurry back to his tomb in the form of a bird with human head, the form given traditionally to souls for these wanderings.

Judgement of the dead

As entry into paradise was a favour, it was only natural that it should entail certain conditions. The most important was that of successfully undergoing judgement.

This had been required since the very beginning by solar doctrine for the official admitted to sharing in the fate of his sovereign. As for Osirian belief, the judgement or pychostasy, is met with in the illustration to Chapter 125 in the Book of the Dead, of which the oldest copies date from the beginning of the eighteenth dynasty, about 1550 B.C.

In the most detailed paintings, Osiris is seated at one end of a hall, under a royal canopy, attended by Isis and Nephtys, having before him a court of forty-two assessors. At the other end, the dead man is brought in by Anubis, the psychopomp or soul leader. A pair of scales is set in the centre of the hall. The heart of the dead man is shown placed on one side, on the other an image or symbol of Maat, goddess of justice. Anubis supervises the weighing and Thot writes the result on his board. A monster shaped like a hippopotamus, the Devourer, is crouching beside the scales, waiting for the damned to be handed over as fodder. The soul who is justified passes through and is led to Osiris by Horus.

The text that goes with this scene is made up of a greeting and the successive declarations of innocence made by the dead man as he comes in to Osiris and his assessors. These are the famous negative confessions. The dead man states that he has not committed a whole series of faults thought of as mortal by the Egyptian conscience. His heart is weighed in order to test his sincerity.

Comparison of the articles of the negative confessions and certain expressions found in the biographical steles from the time of the Old Empire prove that the ethic which they expressed and the judgement of which they were the sanction formed an integral part of Osirian religion from a very early date.

The Book of the Dead is a collection of magic formulas for the use of the dead; it has preserved the text of the negative confessions and the painting of the psychostasy. Undoubtedly, in a context of this sort, the whole would be accepted as being able to work *ex opere operato*, and that recitation of these confessions was thought to enable the dead man, whatever his conduct on earth, to avoid the sanction and make his divine judges believe in his innocence.

Must all the ancient Egyptians therefore be charged with Pharisaism? The compilers of the Book of the Dead were plying their trade as magicians in thus twisting the text of the negative confessions away from so refined an ethic. But it is not so clear that this subterfuge deceived any but those who wished to be, the religious hypocrites that exist in all religions.

The popularity of sapiential literature, which flourished and renewed itself until the very end of Pharaonic civilization, teaching men the true responsibility they have for their acts before God, actually goes to prove the opposite. The manner in which magic gives way to the most lofty moral concepts in the Book of the Dead proves that the latter were common in Egypt. All the dishonesty foisted on the Egyptians by magic, however unpleasant, is an unwilling tribute to their sense of moral uprightness.

TOMBS

Layout of the tombs

The beliefs explained in the foregoing sections found expression in the layout and furnishing of the tombs. The essential part was always the sepulchral chamber, which was sunk deep in the earth, sheltered from all depredations which might destroy the body of the dead man and so prevent his survival as a soul. Here the corpse lay in a sarcophagus, which, from the Old Empire onwards, was almost always a stone urn, made as impregnable as possible. All about it were victuals spread on the ground and ready to eat, with plenty of spare food. These preparations correspond with the conviction that the souls of the dead lived on with their corpses in the tomb.

The dead were supposed to preserve contact with the living through the superstructure of their tombs. In its oldest form this consisted of a mass of rectangular sections supported on all four sides by rough brick walls to which decoration by means of gables gave the look of the façade of a prehistoric palace. An offertory niche, made to look like a door, was set near the south end of the façade, overlooking the Nile. Just behind the offertory niche, now called the false door stele, was a hole leading at first, as in some tombs of the second dynasty, to a shaft, later to a kind of well, and this in turn led to the sepulchral chamber. This was the way the soul went to come out into the world; and also the way by which consecrated offerings were lowered to the dead man in the tomb.

The mastabas of the Old Empire

When the use of stone became general in buildings, brick superstructures were replaced under the Old Empire by stone ones with smooth walls. The huge platform with slightly sloping vertical sides that arose from this treatment has been named "mastaba" in archaeology, an Arabic word meaning "bench". At the same time the false door stele receded further and further into the mass of the superstructure and eventually this brought about a whole set of chambers dedicated to the funerary cult. The mastabas of the fourth dynasty contain no more than a single chamber widened on each side to make the shape of a cross; under the sixth, the mastaba of Mereruka at Sakkara contains no less than twenty-two.

A new phenomenon, which appeared and developed in the mastabas of the Old Empire, was the decoration of their chapels by means of bas-relief and sculpture. The excellent groups of carved walls of Ti or Ptahhotep at Sakkara, for example, are famous. The dead man is seen seated at a table of offerings, receiving the line of servants bringing him the produce of his lands. He is seen, depicted in heroic proportions, looking over the work in the fields in its various seasonal stages and over the workshops of the different trades. He is shown hunting in the marsh, harpooning the hippopotamus or knocking down birds with a boomerang, all amidst great clumps of papyrus.

Though we may admire unreservedly the art responsible for this decoration, we cannot be sure of its most profound significance. Two things are clear: the representation of the dead man sitting down to eat on the transom of the false door expresses pictorially the essential purpose of the rite for which it was intended, the feeding of the departed. The effigies of the dead man carved on the door jambs or in the passages from the several doors of the mastaba, either facing the axis of the stele or turned away from it, illustrate the belief that the dead man could pass freely in and out of the other world by means of this false door.

Apart from this, what interpretation can be given to the other representations? The most generally accepted opinion is that of Maspero who viewed the mastaba decorations as magic pictures which procured in kind for the dead man what they represented pictorially and so enabled him to do without the necessity of material offerings.

The Royal Sepulchres: the Pyramids

The royal tombs of the first two dynasties did not at first differ in any way, except in size, from the tombs of ordinary people. But after the succession of the third dynasty there is a marked difference between royal tombs and others, the former aspiring to a magnificence suitable to the superhuman status of the Pharaohs. Zoser, the founder of the third dynasty in about 2780 B.C., was the first to pile six mastabas of diminishing size one upon the other, for his funeral monument, known as the stepped pyramid of Sakkara, thus opening the way to the grandiose creation which became the typical tomb of the kings of the Old and Middle Empires, namely the pyramid. The steps of Zoser's pyramid symbolize a gigantic stairway, the stairway by which the king mounts to heaven. The architects of Snefru, the first king of the fourth dynasty, c. 2720 B.C., substituted a smooth shape, which better suited the taste for geometrical shapes of this period, demonstrated so powerfully by the monuments of Cheops and Chephren on the plain of Giza.

The most famous of the pyramids, of which there are altogether about seventy-five, are those of the kings of the fourth dynasty, Cheops, Chephren, and Mycerinus, situated on this plain, that of Snefru at Dahshur, and all along the Sakkara desert, those of the kings of the fifth and sixth dynasties.

The symbolism of the ascent of the king, so well expressed by the stairway of the stepped pyramid, was naturally transferred to the smooth pyramid, which was already a solar symbol through its resemblance to the sacred stone of Heliopolis, the *benben* on which, according to legend, the phoenix came to rest. The triangle of its side was interpreted as a drop of light, the last fusion made by rays of the sun with the earth, through which the spirit of the king could rise to the body of the sun itself. In fact, in sculpted hieroglyphs, the rays falling from the sun are shown as a series of little triangles.

Being the inviolable homes of dead Pharaohs, the pyramids inevitably included a place of worship in the form of a temple built on the eastern wall, the inner sanctuary being an architectural rearrangement of the primitive false door. The whole was finished in front by a long covered passage going down to the valley where a reception temple, like that called the Temple of the Sphinx for the pyramid of Chephren, was used as a starting-point for the funeral ceremonies and also the daily worship of the dead king.

The Theban Hypogea

There could be no question of the kings reigning at Thebes starting a field of pyramids, comparable to that which dominated Memphis, around the plain of this city, still less on top of the mountains.

The founders of the eighteenth dynasty solved the difficulty with a stroke of genius. One mountain dominated the Theban massif which, seen at various angles, suggests the shape of a natural pyramid: this is the Holy Mount, adored as a god in this part of the country. The successors of Ahmosis I adopted it as a funeral tumulus. They dug in the deepest of the valleys which wind through its sides, tunnels, which sometimes penetrate, like that of Sethi I, more than three hundred feet into the rock. There, in the place called the valley of the Kings, was the secret, underground part of their tombs, corresponding to the interior passages of the pyramids, and the funeral cells of the mastabas. As there could be no question of making places of worship in this narrow and distant valley in the wilderness, the funeral temples, in which the services for the dead were conducted, were built near the Nile. They were placed along the edge of cultivated land at the desert boundary, and only turned towards the Mount which concealed the royal remains.

For the first time since the remote origins of the Egyptian tomb, the divorce between the underground habitation of the dead and their place of worship was complete.

Syncretism of the Theban tomb

The severance of the connection between the burial place and its temple, that was so thorough in the case of the royal tombs, had no effect on the arrangement of private tombs in the New Empire. The want of space in the necropolis made change impossible and ritual tradition was still vigorous.

The Theban hypogeum for private individuals followed a type which ratified the different developments made in a previous period. Furthermore, this type gave faithful expression to the eclectic beliefs of the time. It had a court, often reached through a small pylon, and at the end of this was the façade of the chapel, carved out of the rock. A small, rough brick pyramid was usually put over the entrance as an expression of faith in solar destiny. On the wall of this façade, facing west, as for Osirian religion, were put offertory steles; one of these was the old false door, the way followed by the soul to come out into the world and an expression of old chthonian beliefs. Within the rock, a hall, placed across the entrance and before a passage running the length of the building and finishing in a cul-de-sac, formed the basic plan of each tomb, more or less developed according to the wealth of the owner. The walls were decorated with paintings, as were the old mastabas, but with modifications to suit the taste of the period and enriched with new scenes. At the end of the passage was either a statue of the dead man, or a false door stele, place above the funeral cell which was reached through a tunnel running from the court for the funeral itself.

EMBALMING AND FUNERAL RITES

The concern, not only to feed the dead man in his grave, but also to preserve his body intact, a *sine qua non*, came from the old chthonian religion of the dead.

The seizure of the soul on the day of burial, before it went down into the funeral cell, formed part of the most ancient funeral rites and had been preserved in the Pharaonic period in the ceremony of the opening of the mouth that was carried out on the mummy. In fact, the primitive Egyptians believed, as do many African peoples to this day, that the soul, freed by death and risking a miserable end in any of several ways, had to be hunted and caught to be forcibly reintegrated with the body by magic rites. But there it lay in a state of inferiority, at the mercy of the good will of the living. The dead man then, restored to life in this way, was quite unable to defend himself from human beings or illness or even to find his own sustenance. His descendants had to do this for him if they did not wish to risk the vengeance of the spirit of the dead man before it too perished.

The ritual requirements for the Egyptian funeral developed from the basic concern to preserve and feed the dead, as did the arrangement of the tomb. Mummification ensured that the dead were preserved, the offertory ceremonies that they were fed.

Mummification

At the beginning of the eighteenth dynasty, the Syrian conquests opened up more fully the Egyptian market for Asian spices. The embalmers took advantage of this to perfect their hitherto rudimentary art. They developed the processes of which the traditions were later recorded by Herodotus and Diodorus of Sicily. The best preserved mummies date from this period, like those in the Cairo Museum, for example, which come from the royal hiding places at Deir el Bahari. This almost perfect art of embalming continued to be practised right up to the end of the Pharaonic civilization. It was only under the Ptolemies that the coarser, but less costly, habit of steeping the corpses in boiling bitumen ousted the old methods until, in the Roman period, it became the only method left.

The corpse treated in this way became identified with Osiris himself. The dead man received in the ritual the title Osiris, a privilege formerly reserved for the kings under the Old

Empire and extended downwards by their descendants: one spoke of so and so's Osiris. Let there be no mistake; there was absolutely no question of identification resulting in a doctrine according to which the personality of the deceased was absorbed by that of the god. Nothing was more foreign to Egyptian thought. It was no more than a legal identification, as elsewhere in funerary and magical literature, the dead man entering into the privileges of Osiris and being thereby supremely safeguarded from his most fearful enemies: the attacks of harmful spirits, and total extinction.

The equipment of a mummy, to be complete, needed at least a coffin, also covered with protective formulas and pictures. Containers, called canopes, in which the entrails of the body were put, were placed by the sarcophagus.

Funerary offerings

The feast served in the chapel of the tomb on the day of burial began a whole series of meals taken to the dead man by the living on the great feast days of the necropolis. But this was not enough to feed the deceased. Like the living they needed daily feeding.

The daily worship of the dead answered this need. It had been practised since the earliest times with offerings of bread and libations of fresh-water made in the temple attached to each tomb. This never prevented the Egyptians from storing victuals in kind by the corpse, sometimes embalmed by the same embalming process to make them last as long as the mummy and often, when their presence had become purely ritual, modelled in glazed earth or sculpted in limestone. However plentiful these items may have been, and they were never very much, except in the mastabas of the Thinite period, they clearly could not possibly suffice the dead man for all eternity. They were never any more than an emergency reserve, a standby. Feeding the dead man was the entire responsibility of the living.

Feeding services in the Necropolis

From the third dynasty onwards, the feeding of the dead

was undertaken for the royal favourites by the monarchs themselves, thanks to the establishment of a royal necropolis. A regular supply of offerings, richly endowed with real estate, fulfilled the needs of all those privileged persons who formed the posthumous court of the Pharaohs buried in the pyramids. The institution functioned regularly for several centuries to the satisfaction of all concerned. The brief formula of the royal privilege granting burial, and solemn and daily offerings, was then carved, as an official mark and sign of glory, on the most obvious places of the chapel.

Magic incantations

However, the time was reached when the impoverished monarchy could no longer bear the weight of the expenditure involved in these funeral services, which had naturally become increasingly heavy with each generation. The provisions became more scanty and the service of the cult, always underpaid, disorganized. The dead were in danger of going hungry.

To avoid this danger, those who possessed tombs thought of appealing to public charity. Inscriptions carved in prominent positions in their chapels promised any visitors who poured libations of fresh water and brought offerings of food for them the benefit of their intercession with the gods.

This was a humiliating request for the great lords to have to make, and all the more so as it seems to have had little or no effect. So magic put in a timely appearance to extract the dead from their difficulty and still preserve their self-respect.

Magical practices had always been latent under the outer show of funeral worship and it had taken the strong, philosophic and social discipline of the Old Empire to purge from it the tombs and their rites by imposing a set of rational and judicial rules on them. As soon as the beneficent omnipotence of the kings who maintained all this beyond the understanding of the masses began to weaken, the magical tradition, dormant for centuries, revived and began to develop with renewed vigour.

It was thereafter admitted that the formula "The King's Favour" which began every edict concerning posthumous privilege, had efficacious power in itself and created such conditions in the next world as it announced in this. It became possible to send the dead all they required by simply reciting a few words. The recitation of formulas beginning with this heading, or even inscribing them in the tomb, became after this period, in the same way as the traditional food rites, the best of all good deeds done for the dead and made up for the lack of material offerings.

Temple endowments

The old practice of letting the souls of the dead share in the offerings made to the king survived, however, the abolishing of the necropolis, but in a new form.

From the Middle Empire onwards, the kings granted to the servants whom they wished to reward the privilege of setting up their own statue in any one of the gods' temples and of dedicating an offertory table to it. After their death, their souls could receive their due of daily sacrifice and benefit, by this roundabout method, from the privilege gained formerly through the raising of statues in the necropolis surrounding the royal pyramid.

CONCLUSIONS

In order to form an impartial judgement on Egyptian religion the question must be viewed as a whole. For us, religion is at once a matter of philosophy and positive belief. Each complements and sustains the other, the first acting as an introduction and motive for the second, this in turn enlightening and perfecting the other.

In ancient Egypt, a philosophical idea of God, pure and strongly founded on tradition, existed from the very beginning of the historic period, and probably well before, alongside a set of positive beliefs which it could not penetrate without overthrowing completely. These beliefs, as we have shown, did not form a homogeneous body of doctrine, but rather a combination of legends originally independent, developed around the various sanctuaries of the cults sanctioned, and even saved from extinction, by the monarchy of the Pharaohs.

In fact, Egyptian thought always tried to order its religious notions and make them fit its philosophical monotheism. The history of Egyptian theology is simply the history of these efforts, which as a whole were doomed to failure. Further, even their partial successes from one point of view could only increase the confusion they aimed to dispel.

In order to adapt the articles of positive religion to the requirements of monotheism, it would, in fact, have been necessary to begin by suppressing all the gods and their cults, as Akh-en-Aton had the courage to do, but tradition, for ever powerful in ancient Egypt, was quite opposed to this revolution which it thought impious. Or at least, if monotheism was prepared to accept a henotheistic compromise (with one great god, supreme over the rest) it would still have been necessary to keep all the other gods in a position of inferiority even in their own temples; here again, tradition was utterly opposed, for every Egyptian god had been considered from time immemorial in his original sanctuary the supreme deity and the true manifestation of the god of current philosophy. So all the efforts of the theologians had only the result of multiplying monotheistic interpretations, in combination with local legends to the advantage of as many gods as had centres of worship in Egypt.

The total effect was increasing confusion in their ideas and terminology, which soon led to despair through a kind of divine pantheism, according to which the gods could all be assimilated to each other and became, in varying degrees, manifestations of the one god.

Finally, it must not be forgotten that Egyptian thought moved in horizons different from ours and that the world to which it belonged did not have the same intellectual disciplines. The prehistoric age, from which it had not shaken itself free, held all these traditions in hallowed respect. And indeed, it was by creating them and keeping them intangible so as to confirm and pass on progress already made, that humanity

had managed to emerge from barbarism and to condemn itself
surely to slip back into it. This exaggerated respect for tradition,
which always held back the development of Egyptian thought,
and blocked its advance, was simply the characteristic of the
old cycle of prehistoric civilization to which other points would
indicate that Egyptian culture still belonged.

PART II

THE ANCIENT RELIGIONS OF WESTERN ASIA

by Georges Contenau

INTRODUCTION

GENERAL OUTLINE

Western Asia, now known as either the Near or the Middle East (of which two terms I prefer the first), included Mesopotamia or the basin of the Tigris and the Euphrates; the lower part was the land of Sumer, the civilization of which spread to the neighbouring parts of the country: to the east, Elam (the south-west of modern Iran), to the north-east, bordered by the Lake Sevan, the kingdom of Urartu or Van, formed more recently than the first, to the north and north-west, Syria and Asia Minor, which later became the sphere of the Hurrite and Hittite powers, to the west, the Mediterranean coast, divided into Phoenicia in the north and Palestine in the south (to which a special study is devoted).

As far back as one may care to inquire, traces are to be found in these areas of a religion based on fertility and fecundity, while all the languages of this vast region are of a particular type, known as agglutinative. This appears sufficiently characteristic to warrant these peoples a special name; they have been called Asianic, a term meaningless in itself but convenient for the purpose of distinguishing them from Semites and Indo-Europeans.

The second group of peoples, the Semites, to whom Arabia is usually ascribed as the homeland, worked its way into the midst of the Asianic peoples and won some of their territory from them, the Lebanon, Upper Syria and North Mesopotamia (Agade or Akkad), well before the historic period. Starting our study in the very beginning, in the third millennium before our era, we find a battle, fought in several stages, between the Sumerians and the Semites of Agade; in the end, during the second millennium, we shall see the Semites triumph over the Sumerians while adopting a more advanced civilization. Though these struggles are the earliest known to us, they are not therefore the oldest; there had certainly been others before, for when the Sumerians first come into view they are already an ancient people with much Semitic admixture, with all the consequences this implies upon civilization and religion. Hence it has always been difficult to draw the line between what is of Sumerian origin, and what belongs specially to the Semites, in Mesopotamian religion. As a guide to the Sumerian element, comparison with other Asianic religions will be useful; likewise with the Semitic element, which we shall compare to the religion of the most ancient Semitic peoples, namely, of their land of origin, in so far as our knowledge of these people permits.

The Indo-Europeans appeared in western Asia at a time when the religions there were already fully formed. But their first known appearance (Hittites, Hurrite contacts) should not lead us to reject the possibility of an earlier appearance, particularly since there is much less difference between the Asianic religions and the religions of the Indo-European group than between the former and Semitic religions, and in the present state of our knowledge influences of one upon the other cannot be ruled out.

Two kinds of sources are available to us: written documents and monuments. Sumerian and, later, Semitic texts give information about worship, liturgy and the pantheon, but whether in Sumer, Akkad or neighbouring kinds, nowhere is there a true exposition of beliefs. The principles of religion were a matter for oral transmission; for those who were familiar with them, all literature devoted to learning, whether religious or profane, was quite clear.

Monuments are the second source; these are legion and the oldest antedate all written sources. But the fact must not be ignored that on many points our knowledge is only conjectural, and whatever we do, we can never penetrate thoroughly the thought of peoples separated from us by several thousands of years. These monuments, the soil of western Asia, unlike Egypt, not having preserved all that was entrusted to it, are temple ruins and decorations, small statues, large ones being almost non-existent, numerous bas-reliefs, small religious objects, even jewellery. Special mention must be made of the "cylinders", used as seals, which have an essentially religious appearance. It must be stressed at the start that the art of ancient western Asia, like Egyptian art, is fundamentally religious; it exists not for its own sake, but to serve religion.

These considerations have determined the plan adopted in our account. We shall first of all describe the Asianic religions least influenced by the Semites, namely those of the Hittites, Hurrites and of Urartu and Elam, then those in which Semitic influence is discernible, the Phoenician and Sumerian, the latter becoming the religion of Babylonia and Assyria. Because of the importance of Mesopotamian civilization, its widespread influence and the knowledge that we have of it we shall devote more space to it than to the others.

1. ASIANIC RELIGIONS

These are naturistic religions, worshipping the principle of fertility and fecundity as expressed by a divine couple, the High god of the mountains, and tempest, the High goddess, and sometimes by the presence, as in human families, of a young god, who has roughly the same attributes as the High god and is represented as the son of the couple.

Feasts fit into the cycle of seasons; the most important is the celebration of the sacred marriage, the hierogamy of the two deities, with all its repercussions on the earth, in the fertility and general fecundity of which it is the symbol.

This state of mind leads to one basic premise: belief, in ancient societies, in the close dependence of the earth on heaven, not only in what this willed, but also in its outward signs.

We encounter these characteristics in what we know of the religion of Hittites and Hurrites, of Urartu and Elam. They are to be seen in the Sumerian religion adopted by the Akkadians, who later became the Assyrians and Babylonians, and also by the Phoenicians, but toned down by their own original beliefs, in Phoenicia as in Mesopotamia.

CHAPTER VI

HITTITES AND HURRITES

HISTORY

The earliest date to which we can trace the Hittites is the second half of the third millennium B.C. In the middle of Asia Minor, in the region of Caesarea of Cappadocia, there are signs of Semitic colonies in the midst of surroundings with Asianic names; these are the Proto-Hittites, in fact the true Hittites, for the later invaders, founders of the Empire (the Hatti) are Indo-Europeans. They united the autochthonous peoples under their rule, flooded Mesopotamia with Semitic colonies and made their capital at Hattusa (now the ruins of Boghaz Köy) in the loop of the River Halys. During the second millennium, the Hatti kingdom was for ever tending to expand out of the poor country in which it was established to conquer more fertile lands. In this they encountered Northern Mesopotamia and, especially, in Phoenicia, the Egyptians, who were engaged in conquering that part of the world. Towards the end of the second millennium the great invasion of "the peoples of the sea" swept away the Hatti empire; later, a few clans of the latter formed a confederation in Syria. This was the New Hittite empire, which Assyria brought to an end in the eighth century B.C.

In the first third of the second millennium, the Hurrites, an Asianic people who had doubtless long been established in Upper Syria, took on a certain importance to the disadvantage of Assyria, founding a short-lived empire, which is known as the Mitanni empire. This foundered under pressure from Assyria about half way through the millennium.

The Hittite language has been known since about 1920; this enables us to decipher many important religious texts discovered in the ruins of Boghaz Köy. The Hurrite tongue, which is less well known, nevertheless gives us some information on the Hurrite pantheon, from which the Hittites borrowed a great deal.

THE PANTHEON

This reflects the composition of the Empire, in that the naturistic gods of the Proto-Hittites rub shoulders in it with those of the Hurrites. It is made up of the gods of different towns: these local cults are complemented by the state cult of worship to the deities of the town of Arinna, near Boghaz Köy, the most important town before Hattusa was founded. These were the sun goddess Wurusemu and her companion the High god, whose animal symbol is the bull. Of other gods, the Proto-Hittite ones were the following: Telepinu, spirit of fertility, Kubaba, who became the Cybebe or Cybele of the Greeks, Santas (the Sandon of Tarsus) and Tarhun in Cilicia (the Etruscan Tarkôn).

The Hurrite gods were Kumarbi, supposedly the father of the heavens, Sauska (analogous to the Babylonian Ishtar), a huntsman god associated with the stag, who ruled the countryside, and above all the divine couple of the goddess Hepat and the god Teshub. To these must be added the gods of the founder dynasty taken from Indian civilization: Mitra, Indra, Varuna and the Nasatyas, and those of Mesopotamia adopted under its influence: Ea, Anu, Enlil and Nergal; it will be readily understood why Hittite treaties are sometimes preceded by the hyperbolical invocation to "the thousand gods" of the kingdom.

But one should not be misled by these "thousand" gods. Many of them refer to the same gods by the different names they bore in the languages of the various clans of the Empire, or even in the same clan under differents aspects. What matters is the fundamental unity of the cult: the sun goddess of Arinna is confused with the High goddess Hepat whose symbol is the

leopardess (or lioness) and also the dove; the High god rules
the atmosphere; he commands the storms, as represented by
the symbols in his hands : the double axe and the thunderbolt
shown as a twisted trident; his animal symbol is the bull, on
which he stands upright.

WORSHIP AND FEASTS

Few Hittite temples are known; it is always necessary to go
back to those at Boghaz Köy, which are linked with large
buildings, giving the impression that they were chapels to a
palace. As we shall see, in Babylonian temples, the statue of
the god was kept at the furthest end of the sanctuary but
visible from the door; in the oldest temple at Ashur the entrance
to the temple, a plain chamber of worship, is on one side
so as to make the statue invisible from the outside; and so it
is in the temples of Boghaz Köy.

The temples were served by priests according to a ritual
which ensured the purification of the celebrants (by ablutions
and special vestments) and governed that of the offerings, fruit,
liquids and animals; the throats of the animals were cut so that
their blood gushed out as a libation poured out before the god.
By definition the king was the high priest, the queen the high
priestess, who could both delegate their powers except in matters
of great importance. The priests acted as servants of the god,
dressing and anointing its statue and bringing offerings of food
and fruit. It was the same in Mesopotamia.

Feasts occurred in accordance with the seasonal round,
especially spring and autumn. One of them included the recitation of the Dragon myth (see below) which may have been
mimed; its purpose was to celebrate and provoke the rebirth of
spring at the end of winter. In all these ceremonies one part
concerned the rôle assigned to the king: his purification, resting, arrival in procession and the ceremonial to reach the position allotted to him, all this interspersed with libation,
censings and sacred songs and dances; some feasts were so
solemn, like the *purulli* in spring, that King Mursil II left his

army in the course of a military campaign in order to come to his capital and celebrate.

DEATH RITES

We know nothing about the ceremonies carried out at the death of a private individual; for a king they lasted at least thirteen days. The body was burnt, the bones anointed with oil and wrapped in a cloth; all was then put on a stand and offerings of food made before it. After a symbolic meal and sacrifice the bones were placed on a couch in the innermost room of the "stone house". At Boghaz Köy few traces of incineration have been found; there are many of inhumation carried out in the earth beneath the houses. O. R. Gurney, who has described these practices, points out what they have in common with the Homeric ceremonies, in that these include funeral games, while the Hittite ones are accompanied by magical acts.

DIVINATION AND MAGIC

Like all the peoples of early antiquity, the Hittites practised both, and a further example will be seen in the Sumerians; we need only mention the fact that the Hittites consulted the oracles obtained by examining the entrails of sacrificed victims, the flight of birds and a form of divination of which we know nothing, practised by old women and called simply "the Old Women" in the texts. When the matter was important, the soothsayers fixed the conditions; several successive examinations took place, an affirmative or negative answer being attached to them according to whether they were favourable or not.

Magic played an important part in ritual; it was used for regaining health, for dispersing evil spirits, and to attract the good intentions of the powerful or the gods. When directed against one's neighbour (black magic), it was prosecuted by the law.

MYTHS

Again, like other peoples of the Near East, the Hittites explained their beliefs indirectly by means of myths. The best known are those of Telepinu and the killing of the Dragon.

Telepinu is the spirit of vegetation. When he went to sleep in the winter, the gods were upset by his absence; things were not increasing any more, vegetable nor animal, and foodstuffs had lost their nutritive value. The gods began the search and he was found, but fast asleep; the bee was sent to sting him and wake him up, and to give him strength by rubbing him with her wax. It is generally recognized in folklore that bee stings can cure paralysis and that honey is a purifying agent.

The Dragon's death myth was recited or sung at the New Year feast (as in Mesopotamia with the recital of the killing of Tiamat). The dragon, Illuyanka, symbol of the powers of evil, was the enemy of the High god. Following the god's advice, a goddess invited it to a meal; it arrived with its young, became drunk and bloated itself with food and was unable to go back into its cave. Advantage was taken of this to bind it with rope, whereupon the High god killed it (just as Marduk slew Tiamat).

IMAGES OF THE GODS

As Hittite art was fundamentally religious, there are plenty of representations or symbols of the deities. In the first period of Hittite history these mostly take the form of simplified little idols of the mother goddess and medals showing the animal symbols of the High god, bull and stag. In the second millennium, wonderful material is provided in the rock-side carvings of an open air temple at Yazilikaya near Boghaz Köy. These are ascribed to the thirteenth century B.C., K. Bittel placing them in the fifteenth century as far as the main subject is concerned. Two processions are shown advancing towards each other, one of gods and the other of goddesses; the gods wear short tunics, conical mitres and ride their symbolic animals; the High god is standing on the shoulders of two kings who are doubtless deities of the mountains which he frequents; most of these gods carry their symbols or their names in hieroglyphs in their hands. The High goddess is standing on a leopardess or lioness; she wears a long robe and cylindrical tiara; next comes the son god, standing on a mount like that of the High goddess and carrying a double-headed axe. Elsewhere he is clasping the shoulders of a king dressed in high priestly robes; this is Tudalia IV who reigned during the last period of the empire (second half of the thirteenth century B.C.). At Malatia, in eastern Asia Minor, a series of bas-reliefs shows the king or queen pouring a libation before various gods. One of the sculptures from this source shows the Dragon being killed, not by a trick but in a straight fight. The Dragon is shown as a serpent which the god is lancing, at the same time dropping thunder bolts and large hailstones on to the monster. These representations are examples of the richness of the scenes featuring the gods which are reproduced in most works on Hittite art. The variants of some myths, a feature also of Babylonian mythology, postulate a common source treated by different religious centres.

URARTU

Only short mention is made here of the religion of Urartu, a kingdom that flourished to the north of Lake Van and became very important during the Assyrian hegemony. It withstood the attacks of the Sargonids to be finally overthrown by the Scythians at the beginning of the sixth dynasty B.C. Little is known of its religion, which was Asianic. Beside its chief god Khaldi, the god Teshub gave his name to the town of Tesheba, near modern Erivan, nowadays the site known as Karmir Blur.

ELAM

The religion of south-western Iran, which was called the land of Elam, belongs to the same group as the foregoing religions, but the closeness of the religious metropolises of

Mesopotamia exerted great influence on it, especially in the composition of its pantheon which puts Mesopotamian gods right next to Elamite ones. The chief national god was Inshushinak, "The Lord of Susa", this name being written with the hieroglyph for "cedar", a species which disappeared in Elam at about the beginning of the historic age. Then there was the god Huban, and his attendant goddess Kiri Risha and in the south, the god Gal and goddess Urbukubak, couples which symbolized the forces of fertility and fecundity. The temples, now destroyed, were decorated with low reliefs in moulded brick which showed, among other things, the sacred tree guarded by the genii, secondary deities who carried a jar to gushing waters.

One bronze monument, discovered in a hiding place, showed a religious ceremony with two celebrants and, on a smaller scale, two storeyed towers, offerings, jars of water for ablutions, the sacrificial hall and a few small trees as the sacred grove to go with the temple buildings. All the monuments at Susa were completely destroyed by Asshurbanipal, in about 640 B.C., who boasts of having ruined its ziggurat (or storeyed tower). Ghirshman, who is in charge of the digging at Susa, has uncovered at Choga Zanbil near Susa, the remains of a ziggurat with constructional details differing from the Mesopotamian form. A few texts from Susa seem to allude to the possibility of retribution in a future life and there is also a prehistoric necropolis which gave us one of the most beautiful pieces of funeral ceramic art of all antiquity.

CHAPTER VII

PHOENICIA

Until a few years ago, Phoenician religion was only known through the ancient authors, Herodotus and his successors, the references in the Old Testament and the Homeric poems which described Phoenicia in its period of splendour. Its geographical position makes it the link between Egypt and Asia, exposing it to the invasions of its powerful neighbours and, in the late period, to Greek and Roman influences. The writings of this last period provided the basis of all our knowledge. Philo of Byblos, who lived at the beginning of the Christian era, has handed down Phoenician beliefs about the creation of the world as according to one Sanchuniathon, a priest born at Beryta (Beirut) in about the eleventh century B.C. His work is lost, Philo's being only partly preserved by Eusebius of Caesarea, who wrote at the beginning of the fourth century A.D. All this information has been much discussed and sometimes doubted. In any case, it offered a picture very different from what primitive religion must have been.

Since 1919 the situation has been changed by the successive excavations by Montet, Virolleaud and Dunand at Byblos, the modern Jebail north of Beirut, and at Ra's Shamra, the ancient Ugarit, near Latakia, where Schaeffer uncovered numerous tablets inscribed with cuneiform characters, but of a system simpler than the Mesopotamian, the writing being alphabetic. This writing was deciphered by H. Bauer, E. Dhorme and C. Virolleaud, the last of whom translated the texts which reveal the nature of primitive Phoenician religion: a religion of Asianic type, rich in myths of epic form, which can be traced to as far back as King Niqmad (fourteenth century B.C.). Whereas an overall view is possible for the first millennium, for the previous period the discoveries at Byblos for Phoenicia and of Ra's Shamra for the north alone provide any information. We shall deal with each in turn.

At Byblos, which because of its nearness to Egypt was brought under its influence, there were found some old Egyptian texts which refer to a god, Hay-Tau, who was metamorphosed into a fir tree. This reference likens this god to Osiris, whose body, according to legend, was surrounded and enclosed in the wood of a tree, and also to Adonis, spirit of vegetation and the tree. The Pharaoh Pepi I, in a funerary inscription, compares himself in his wooden coffin to the god Hay-Tau. The temple of Byblos which was rebuilt after 2000 B.C. had, until the Roman period, three consecutive courts leading to a flagged square, the door of which was flanked by statues of the gods, if indeed the sanctuary has been correctly reconstructed; a second temple, discovered in 1939, had succeeded an earlier building and included a fore-court, a court enclosing the sanctuary and a series of little obelisks. Egyptian influence in religion is patent in this area.

The oldest type of Phoenician tomb is represented at Byblos. It is an aeneolithic hypogeum in hollowed out caves where bodies were placed folded up in large jars and provided with very simple grave appointments, weapons and food containers. More recent are two princely tombs dating from the twelfth Egyptian dynasty; the tombs of two princes of Byblos. A tunnel has been dug from the tomb to the surface so as to enable the soul of the dead man to come out. Still more recent is the tomb of King Ahiram of Byblos, a contemporary of Ramses II, his overlord. On one of its sides the sarcophagus reproduces the women weeping at his funeral. Such tomb offerings as have escaped the robbers reflect, in the same way as in Egypt, the necessity felt for providing the dead man with all he needed for his life in the next world.

THE GODS

At Ra's Shamra, El-Dagon, whose duty it is to rule rivers

and wells, is the head of the pantheon; his associate-goddess is Asherat of the sea, also known as Elat, the feminine of the word El, which just means "God". Next is his son, the god Baal (meaning "master") who corresponds to the Mesopotamian Adad and the Syrian Hadad, god of the mountain tops, the storm and the rain. Associated with him is Asherat (not to be confused with Asherat of the sea). The son of Baal, Aliyan, has certain attributes which in some respects are merely a duplication of his father's powers, a common feature in Asianic religion. While the animal symbol of Baal is the bull, that of Aliyan is the caprid (goat). Anat, Aliyan's sister, is a warrior goddess who was adopted by the Egyptians. The antagonist of Aliyan is his brother Mot, whose name means the "Hero" or, as some would have it, "Death", and he has the characteristics of the midday sun, which dries everything. So the series is complete: the High god and goddess, the son god Aliyan who rules springs and rivers, and Mot, his brother, symbolizing the harvest and the succeeding sleep of nature.

This is all expressed in various myths: in that of Baal and Aliyan, Baal's task leads to that of Mot, whom the goddess Anat kills at harvest time. The death of Mot is described as the death of an ear of corn, cut and crushed to flour. He must make way for Aliyan who will reappear somewhat later to presage the renewal; then the cycle continues; the two brothers cannot stay on earth together, and one must be below ground when the other reigns. This myth illustrates the traditional land rite of the "last sheaf". Among other poems on the same subject, the "Hymn to the goddess Nikkal and the goddesses Kosharot" includes the description of the sacred marriage, the hierogamy of the gods, which forms part of the fertility rites.

Also to this period belong the remains of two temples, close to each other and identical in plan, as one is consecrated to Dagon and the other to his son Baal. The temple consisted of a court with an altar raised on two steps; behind is a *pronaos* and *naos* of which one side was a kind of platform for the image of the god or for placing offerings. The god El-Dagon, father of Baal, is given by this a naturistic character confirmed by his second name of Dagon, meaning "grain". Only later was the nature of a sea-god wrongly ascribed to him because of the Semitic meaning of the word Dagan, "fish"; the first and true nature of Dagon is certainly agricultural, seeing that he also had the surname of Siton, meaning "corn".

The tombs of Ra's Shamra, which resulted from Hyksos and later Mycenean influence, were dug under the houses, or very close to them; a stairway led to a little passage which opened on to a rectangular cellar with dry stone walls somewhat at an angle and a roof of flag stones, either flat or cantilevered. One part of the tomb was kept for liquid offerings or else water was poured down into it through pipes. Evidently, then, belief in material existence in the next world was part of the religion of Ra's Shamra.

REPRESENTATIONS OF THE GODS

The god El is shown on an offertory stele; he wears a belted robe, has a beard, long hair and horned tiara on his head. Baal is represented on a tall limestone stele in the Louvre, dressed as a warrior in a short loin cloth, bearded, his hair spreading out over his shoulders, and wearing a tapering, cap-shaped helmet. In one hand he wields a club and in the other a lance, with point downwards, the other end dividing up into many florid branches, probably the symbol of the storm, which rains on the vegetation and causes its rebirth. Aliyan is dressed like Baal, and wears shoes with slightly raised points. He holds the Egyptian hooked sceptre. He is beardless and in front of his headdress is a tall, slightly curved leaf, looking like a plume. Another sort of deity reproduces a very ancient prototype. It appears as a flat idol clad in a very short loin cloth, with protruding nose, and jutting arched eyebrows. Idols of the goddess show her naked, embossed on a metal plate. One of them shows her standing on a lion which has a star-shaped rosette on its shoulder; this is the symbol of the Mesopotamian goddess Ishtar, who has all the characteristics of the High goddess.

During the following period, the Phoenician gods lost some

of their features and acquired others. The large towns worshipped a city patron; in Tyre this was Melqart, assimilated to Heracles by the Greeks. Originally a purely solar god, he added the attribute of marine divinity, but his ancestry should not be lost sight of. He is the son of Zeus, the High god. Dagon, mentioned in the Ra's Shamra texts, is not lost but, through his marine features, becomes identified by some with the Babylonian Oannes, half man, half fish. Reshef is assimilated to Apollo and, at Sidon, where the ruins of his temple can still be seen, there reigned Eshmun, identified with Asklepios, a chthonian health god. These gods such as Melqart and Reshef are graded as lords and masters and, like the naturistic High god, are characteristically solar deities. Female deities, or Baalats (feminine of Baal), were worshipped at Beirut and Byblos where they were confused with Ashtart the High goddess, mother goddess and personification of fecundity; the Sidonians revered her as well. Her cult is closely connected with that of Adonis, who is found again in Mesopotamia under the name of Tammuz. He figures prominently in naturistic pantheons; we have seen him as Telepinu with the Hittites, as Aliyan at Ugarit. Damascius in the sixth century A.D. was familiar with his true character and likens him to Eshmun, or Adonis, by another name, just as Baal was applied to the High god. This cult, then, goes back to the dawn of history, tying up with the worship of Hay-Tau in the third millennium. We have an Egyptian cylinder seal of this period showing the Lady of Byblos on it as Isis Hathor beside Hay-Tau, as found much later.

Everything points to the complete acceptance by antiquity of the cult of the High god and High goddess. The Phoenician pantheon is that of a primitive, early Asia, but with the modifications caused by the spreading of a single cult over vast areas.

Alongside these gods, mountains, rivers and some trees are objects of worship, not as gods, but as their places of residence at times: the Baals of Lebanon and Hermon, the river Adonis with its sanctuary dedicated to Ashtart, the river Asklepios

in Sidon and the sacred woods of the temples are examples.
Connected with that cult of stones is the "betyl" cult, this
being a transcription of a Semitic word meaning "abode of the
deity". Betyls are upright stones, as in the temples of Byblos
and Gezer, between Jaffa and Jerusalem. It is conjectured that
these bear the same relation to Ashtart as the little wooden
column, the *asherah*, found so frequently in temples, bears to
Adonis.

Except the temples of Ra's Shamra, Phoenician sanctuaries
were often "High places", consecrated spaces open to the sky
on hills with a small chapel or betyl in the centre. These are
comparable to the thrones of the gods carved or sculpted in
the rocks of the mountains in Asia Minor, at Kara Dagh.

A large staff was attached to the great temples, like those
of Byblos, which was responsible for sacrifices, among other
duties. A tariff of sacrifices found at Marseilles, composed in
the third century B.C., gives us the economic picture. It shows
what fell to the sacrificer and the offerer for all types of sacrificial animals, whether calf, ram, goat, lamb, bird or libations.

The feast of Adonis was celebrated at Afka in the summer
and was attended by worshippers from Byblos and all over
Phoenicia. It was divided into two distinct parts, firstly general
lamentation and then universal joy for the resurrection of the
god. Though evidence for the details of Phoenician festivals is
slight, what we have for Alexandrian festivals of the second
century B.C. enables us to reconstruct the principal outlines of
this festival. As will be seen, it is much the same in Mesopotamia with the disappearance of Tammuz.

For the soul of a dead man, the life of the other world was
joyless and vegetative, dependent on the fate of the body it
had animated. The dead man needed offerings and rest too in
his eternal abode. Hence the care taken to hide the graves in
the bottom of well-nigh inaccessible wells, a care well justified
by the boldness of the tomb robbers. The dead were not in-
cinerated but placed in sarcophagi, the shape of which changed
as time went by. In the first millennium, they were sometimes the

theca, or chests with hog backed lids, or sometimes sarcophagi, called anthropoid because of the imitation of the outline of a body and the human head in relief on the lid; this is the Egyptian mummy reproduced in marble and was used mostly during the Persian period. After this, Greco-Roman styles are followed.

There are not many important representations of gods in this second period; two steles are worthy of mention: of Baal at Amrit which shows traces of most varied influence. The beardless god, wearing the royal Egyptian headdress, holds a small lion by the hind paws in one hand and wields a scimitar in the other. He is dressed in a belted tunic with one flap floating behind; he is standing on a lion, which itself is on mountainous ground and the winged solar disk dominates the whole scene. The Byblos stele shows the king, dressed in Persian style, standing in prayer before the Baalat of Byblos, who wears Egyptian costume, with a wig over which is the disk between two horns; that is the goddess Hathor. Here, the character of the primitive gods persists but their costume is derived from several sources, Egyptian, Assyro–Babylonian and Hittite.

MORAL VALUE OF PHOENICIAN RELIGION

Originally steadfastly naturistic in all manifestations, the nature of the gods, their dress and mythology, Phoenician religion remains so in the Greco-Roman period, but the characteristic features must be sought beneath the modifications brought about by the foreign influences that it underwent all the time. The Phoenicians had the conception of gods who were masters, but good ones, and of the idea of justice and good in itself. During the Persian period they showed a sentiment of wide-embracing responsibility when the king who dedicated the stele of Byblos asks the goddess "to let him live, to lengthen his days and years, for he is a just king, and to make him acceptable in the eyes of the gods and of his people".

Unfortunately, and the Orient is not exempt from these contrasts, those aspirations are found together with the practice of human sacrifice inherited from the ancient Canaanites, notably of first-born children, as is proved by the discovery at Carthage of urns placed in tiers containing their bones, and also, at Kafer Jarra, near Sidon, of the remains of a foundation sacrifice of the same nature.

2. MESOPOTAMIA

We now come to deal with the religion of ancient Mesopotamia. The principal features of the Asianic religions of the neighbouring countries, described in the preceding chapters, will be seen to be present in the Sumerian religion where, however, they had been modified from the earliest times by previous contact between the Sumerians and the Semitic peoples.

CHAPTER VIII

SUMERIAN RELIGION

There are two successive phases in Mesopotamian religion, the Sumerian and the Babylonian, corresponding to the two great periods of Mesopotamian history. In the first, the land of Sumer, which includes the low countries, spreads its civilization throughout the Tigris and Euphrates Basin and extends it more or less into the surrounding lands. In about 2800 B.C. it is in full splendour and lasts after this until the Semites living in the western part called the Amurru, after a struggle, sometimes to their advantage, put an end finally to the Sumerian predominance and founded the first Babylonian Dynasty, about 2000 B.C. We observe first the development of the Sumerian power, the struggles in every town to form a coherent state. A first arrival of the Semites of Akkad for a time denied supremacy to the Sumerians (twenty-fifth to twenty-third centuries). The latter regained it indirectly when the barbarous mountain tribes of the Zagros destroyed the empire of Agade, and, after a century of rule, were themselves driven out by the Sumerians.

This ushered in the Neo-Sumerian period of the third dynasty of Ur (twenty-second to twenty-first century) which itself came to an end under the combined attacks of the Semites and Elamites from the south-east of the Mesopotamian plain where they had been in contact with the tribes of the Iranian plateau. Under the two dynasties of Isin and Larsa the transition to a complete return of Semitic power was effected.

This is the outline of the history for these first centuries but it would be a mistake to think that Sumerian religion had not earlier undergone the influence of its neighbours in the land of Akkad. From the very beginning this religion was fundamentally Asianic but was still not without traces of Semitism; it is extremely difficult to define Sumerian religion in its purest form. In the third dynasty of Ur especially, the Neo-Sumerians took pains to collect together the treasures of their religious past. For the pre-Akkadian period we make use of the contemporary inscriptions and monuments.

Fortunately, although we have no written sources for the proto-historic period, i.e. the period immediately preceding the historic, we can make use of figured monuments which enable us to distinguish with fair certainty the main features of Sumerian religion in the Jemdet Nasr period, so called after a site in central Mesopotamia, and, before this, in the Uruk period (modern Warka), Uruk being the name of the metropolis in the south of the land of Sumer.

At Warka, since the Uruk period, during the fourth millennium B.C., there existed the "terrace temple", the forerunner of the "storeyed tower" and other sanctuaries, long and quadrilateral in shape, having a cella at one narrow end facing the entrance, and large rooms on each side, doubtless for ritual purposes. These temples were decorated with bright colours, red and white, sometimes inlaid with coloured terra cotta, making a mosaic.

On the same site near the Persian Gulf, for the Jemdet Nasr period (end of fourth millennium to beginning of third) German digs uncovered a stone vase just over three feet tall, decorated with a procession divided into four horizontal bands. The goddess, in a long robe, is standing before a sacred enclosure set aside for the offerings, marked by her symbol, two bunches of reeds, the knotted upper ends of which are left free to wave; these are the stakes which stood on either side of dwellings in the primitive period. On the other side of these staves are the offerings already received, a ram, baskets of fruit, vases like the one we are just describing, statuettes of animals with bowls on their backs for scent and incense, and other statuettes. A file of worshippers is approaching the goddess in a state of ritual nudity, and bearing presents. Unfortunately, opposite the goddess, the person leading the procession is missing through a breakage. There is only the bottom of his robe and the end of his girdle held by one of the porters. This must be the god, identified by the remaining piece of belt, one of his attributes. The god is introducing himself for the sacred marriage, the hierogamy, a rite essential to fertility cults; of the last two bands one is filled with animals offered to the goddess, rams and sheep, the other with a frieze of stylized barley ears and palm branches, both divine symbols.

There are contemporary replicas of this scene on the cylinder seals for sealing tablets: either the god dressed in the same robe holding flowered branches out to caprids, or the god and goddess together, the god holding an ear (of barley), the goddess her symbolic curved staff; or the god may be coming forward between two porters, one bearing his collar, or a collar to be offered to the goddess, the other the same belt as on the above-mentioned vase.

This theme, with all its variations, is one of the commonest of the carvings of this period and there can be no doubt as to its meaning.

It is possible to infer that such a religion existed in Mesopotamia even during earlier, prehistoric periods. The recent digs on the Jarmo site (east of Kerkuk) which were started before

Hassuna (south-west of Nimrod) have produced, for the period dating to before 4000 B.C., statuettes of the mother goddess in rough earth, which foreshadow the statuettes of goddesses with snake-like heads, sometimes holding a child in their arms, found on the Ur site for the archaic period.

The other deities in the pantheon are the result of a union of the patrons of different cities. The goddess is often worshipped under different names: Inanna, "the Lady of the Sky", Nintud, Ninhursag, Nidaba, grain goddess, Geshtina, "celestial vine". The High god and young god preserve their identities under the forms of Ningirsu, who controls the flood, of the town of Lagash (modern Tello), of the god Shara, meaning greenness, of the town of Umma, near Lagash, and the god Abbu, father of vegetation; we may also mention Sumuqan, god of cattle, Ningizzida, "lord of the wood of life", and Dumuzi-Apsu, "legitimate son of the void", a shepherd who became king, then god, before the flood; whose father was Enki, the god of the abyss of sweet, fertilizing waters, on which the earth floats. This religion is quite coherent; the multiplicity of the divine names should not mislead. They are but different aspects of the great principle of fertility and fecundity which can be recognized in their emblems: the ear of corn, the vase whence water gushes out and the lion-headed eagle holding the caprids.

With the beginning of history these names became less frequent; representations of the gods change their character, but at bottom the primeval divine nature is not missing from the new entities: Anu, father of the gods and supreme generator, Enki, lord of the soil and of the watery underground, Enlil, god of wind and rain, Utu, the sun, not the midday sun which dries everything up, but the morning sun which aids plant growth. Nanna, the moon god, is lord of the sky. However these gods are the sign of a broadening of the pantheon which must be due to the Semites; this is indicated by their distinguishing determinatives, the star signifying "god", and the fact that the sky is their home. On the other hand, the cylinder seal carvings continue to represent fertility divinities; sometimes their bodies give birth to branches, sometimes they hold boughs as worshippers; among their symbols are the snake, a chthonian animal, the bull, symbol of generation forces like the ram, the sheaf of corn, the plough; under the third dynasty of Ur, the vase from which a cascade of water escapes, known as the "vase of gushing waters", becomes a characteristic emblem of the gods. The cylinder-seal of Gudea, of this period, shows the dynast presented by his patronal god Ningizzida to Ningirsu, the chief god of the town. The latter's emblem is the vase of gushing waters repeated several times; snake heads come forth from the shoulders of Ningizzida.

TEMPLES

At first a plain room with the entrance on one side, benches inside for the offerings and an altar for the image of the god (as in the oldest temple of Assur, dedicated to Ishtar), but at Warka, as early as the Uruk period, the temple takes the form of a long room with the door at one end, the altar at the other opposite it; the interior is divided into cella and antecella.

It was in the temples that communal prayers, lamentations, music and sacred dances and the all-important sacrifices took place. Here also the wish of the gods was consulted by divination, demons were overcome by magic, and here, besides the daily worship, the ceremonies of the great feasts were performed.

But the temple is not merely that. The Sumerians, after creating their gods in man's image, built for them a home equal to the king's palace, furnishing it and endowing it with servants and domestic animals. One of the recensions of the epic poem of the hero Gilgamesh of Uruk relates his meeting with the goddess Ishtar; when he comes out of the royal palace with his friends he finds himself before the goddess who has come out of her temple with a retinue of priestesses. The difference is that Gilgamesh is bound to the earth, while Ishtar can return at will to the sky to see her father, Anu. So, conforming to custom, when Gudea builds a temple to his god, he does not omit to make it like a palace, nor to provide him with a domestic retinue of servants, musicians, chariots and beasts to draw them; after this he puts in the god and goddess for their sacred marriage, the fount of earthly goods.

From prehistoric times, the Sumerian buried his dead either beneath his house or in cemeteries, with the funerary offerings for his other-world existence. These offerings had to be renewed by his family, notably the son, who is known as the "oil burner", i.e. the one responsible for the funeral cult. The so-called "royal" tombs at Ur, which date from the beginning of history, and the only ones to be found intact, present the spectacle of the sacrifice of the whole court of a king and another of a queen: guards, harem and courtiers; the chariots were buried together with all the trappings and the charioteer, and all round is a profusion of gold and jewels. Among those in the tomb of the queen, many are shaped ornamentally as pomegranates, bulls, stags, and ears of corn, unmistakable reminders of fertility cults.

SUMERIAN MYTHS

These were often reshaped by the Semites in the course of time and sometimes only the reshapings have survived; more often, the Sumerian poem has served as a starting point and has been greatly modified; sometimes it is toned down and loses its primitive flavour the better to correspond with the taste of the period in which it is revised. It is remarkable that the number of poems written in Semitic and thought to have no prototype is diminishing as more discoveries are made; often the Sumerian original is found. This was the case with the poem of Gilgamesh, of the myth of Adapa, and the tale of the hierogamy of gods which before was thought to be about "the Fall of Man". In this text, the gods, spirits of fertility, are identified with nature itself; the god becomes a cosmic force and impregnates the marsh with his vital power, and the goddesses who come to it bear fruit from it if, that is, the translation of the poem, which has had several other versions, expresses its real meaning.

3. BABYLONIA AND ASSYRIA

The complete control gained by the Semites over the land of Sumer under the first Babylonian dynasty was the consequence of a long process of infiltration. In the north-west of Mesopotamia, among the peoples in contact with the Asianics, were the Amorites, whose name means "people of the west". When the Agadeans, after a century and a half of rule, which was not without its effect, were ousted by the third dynasty of Ur, Amorite pressure was continued, but peacefully, through the settlements made by these foreigners whose proper names appear everywhere in records of transactions. They become an integral part of the population; later, they take advantage of the Elamite attack which terminated Neo-Sumerian rule and founded the kingdom of Larsa to found their own new kingdom of Isin, the name, like Larsa, being taken from the city chosen as capital. About 2000 B.C. a third kingdom, Babylon, is set up; co-existing for more than a hundred years with the other two, it finally absorbed them, after they had been fused together, in the reign of Hammurabi (1792–1750 B.C.). Proper names became Semitic and so did the language, Akkadian, from which both Babylonian and Assyrian later developed; the names of office also, and when Babylonian had no terms to clothe a Sumerian expression, it took over the Sumerian term and adapted it to Babylonian form. The Babylonians did not replace Sumerian in everything by their own language. They took over Sumerian civilization but preserved the language as a sacred tongue, a kind of liturgical language. This respect for the past is part of the oriental character; as is the respect of the nomad for settled peoples and the facility with which the Semites adapted from one civilization what was lacking in their own. The Amorites brought

with them an underdeveloped religion; they adopted the
Sumerian and reshaped it a little; but it must not be supposed
that the religion of Babylon was a contribution of the invaders
nor must Sumerian and Semitic religions be contrasted. The
Amorites left their mark and infused their spirit, but what
finally prevailed, except in small details, was the religion of
Sumer. The original religion of Mesopotamia was never lost
sight of, and comparison of religious texts with those of the
third dynasty of Ur proves that the differences are more formal
than essential.

The first dynasty of Babylon did much for the establishment
of the religion which easily survived the waves of political
upheaval and maintained its original character almost up to
our own era. The invasion of more mountain tribesmen from
the Zagros, the Kassites, during the second millennium, only
modified it by the addition of a few of the invaders' gods which
disappeared along with them. The Persian domination had no
effect; the Hellenizing conquests of Alexander and the Seleucids
drew a transitory veil over the local religion without obscuring
it, and paradoxically enough, some of the most complete texts
we have to describe the ceremonies then celebrated in the
temples of Babylon date from this period. Before dealing with
the actual description of the religion, we shall say a few words
on Mesopotamian thought without which some of their beliefs
would remain quite obscure.

We owe this term "Mesopotamian" to E. Pottier, who taught
at the Ecole du Louvre during the first years of the century:
he adopted it in his lectures for all he found common to the
civilization of the Sumerians and of the Semites after them and
popularized its use through his writings.

Among the special peculiarities of Mesopotamian thought in
the ancient period, we shall first mention what may be called
the "Doctrine of Names", which can be expressed in this
axiom: all that exists has a name, what has no name does
not exist. The Egyptians thought in the same way and this belief
led them to establish a close link between the object or the
individual and its name and think that knowledge of the name

of something gave power over it, and to name it was to appropriate it and straightway to realize whatever was desired concerning it. Hence the Egyptians hid their real names so as to escape from outside control. But this power of the word, provided that it was spoken in a tone suitable to what it expressed, is only temporary. A prayer only affects a god while it is actually pronounced, if written down it has lasting power, and is greatly beneficial if written on a statue of the believer which openly bears his name. The gesture which went with the word, the power of which was doubled by mime, led to sacred dances, just as the word reinforced by song gave rise to prayers sung in common. This belief in the value and power of names gradually came to have the most widespread results. We shall see later how the Babylonians imagined the universe, but, as has been mentioned, we know that they placed the dwellings of their gods in the sky; they believed that a prayer said in the proper way automatically effected the god's action; imagining the world of heaven to be like what they saw on earth, they believed, like the Sumerians, in an interdependence of sky and earth, and that any act committed in one of the two spheres had its repercussions in the other. With the oriental mind reasoning as much by analogy as by deduction and induction, the notion of one act or thing recalling another in such a way as to evoke it and even to equal it, led them to the idea of symbol, for which they everywhere found applications.

CHAPTER IX

HEAVEN AND THE GODS

THE PANTHEON

The great gods of the Sumerian pantheon, who had already to
some extent supplanted the fertility gods of the Asianic cults,
hold the highest position; only the most important can be
mentioned here. First is Anu, as in Sumer, god of the sky, a
rather unobtrusive character, but nevertheless continually
honoured up to the end of the Seleucids at Uruk, in the Eanna,
"sky temple"; he is rarely represented and then only by a
horned tiara, his symbol. As "Father of the gods", Enlil, god
of wind and storm, takes the name of Bel, "lord"; he is
worshipped in the town of Nippur, in the Ekur, "mountain
temple"; his symbol is the tiara, as for Anu. His associate goddess is sometimes Ninlil and sometimes Ninhursag, "Mountain
Lady". Ea, "the Water Abode", is the Sumerian Enki, god of
the soil and the underground; he is called creator of the world.
He is honoured at Eridu, the holy city of the south in the
Eabzu, "temple of Apsu", the ocean on which the world rests.
He is the master of rites and of all knowledge. He is shown
surrounded by waves with his symbol, a kid, the hind quarters
being a fish-tail. Associate goddesses: Damkina, "wife of the
sky and the earth", Damgalnunna, "Great wife of the Prince",
Mah, "the Sublime one". Ishtar, a product of Semitic syncretism, unites three personalities: goddess of battles, of love (by
absorption into the Sumerian Inanna) and goddess of the
planet Venus. She represents the ancient naturistic cult with the
greatest intensity in one of her aspects. Several Sumerian deities
were assimilated to her. She is shown either as a warrior god-

dess or naked; her symbol, depending on each case, is the lion, the dove, or the star. Sin, the moon god (Sumerian Nannar), worshipped at Ur; under the third dynasty of Ur, his cult spread to Harran in the north. He is "Master of the Crown" (the crescent moon); he is a god willing to give help and his image is that of a man of mature age accompanied by a crescent moon; his associate goddess is Ningal, the "Great Lady". Shamash, the sun god (Utu in Sumerian), son of Sin, is the god of justice who sees all things. Worshipped in the Ebabbar "Sun temple", he is shown enthroned with the solar disk as an attribute; sometimes rays spread out from his shoulders; his associate is Aya, who later becomes an Ishtar. Adad originated in the west where he is called Hadad, an Amorite god who becomes important under the first Babylonian dynasty. Master of the wind and the rain, like the Baal of Ra's Shamra, his associate goddess is Shala. He is represented standing on a bull. Nergal is the god of Hell, in Sumerian euphemistically called Ne-unugal, "Domination of the Great Abode". First worshipped at Kutha and represented as a slaughterer god, his associate goddess is Ereshkigal, "Princess of the Great Earth", known as Allatu by the Semites. Marduk, probably, but not certainly, of Sumerian origin, was the god of Babylon and under the first dynasty became the state god. He is the eldest son of Ea and received the "dignity of Enlil", i.e. supremacy over the gods. At Babylon his main temple was the Esagil "Lofty headed Temple". Associate goddess: Sarparnit "the Shining". The son of Marduk is the god Nabu of Borsippa near Babylon; he is worshipped in the Ezida, "Temple of Fidelity". God of *belles lettres*, he is the scribe of the fates in the Assembly of the gods. Gradually, he nearly supplanted Marduk, just as the latter had taken on the powers of his father, Ea. His associate is a hypostasis: Tashmetum, "Intelligence", sometimes Nidaba, goddess of cereals, but also she who "knows the numbers".

Among other gods less frequently met with are: Amurru, in Sumerian Martu, god of "the West", or of the Great Mountain; his symbol is the caprid and he is analogous to Adad

(the Baal of Ugerit). His associate is Ashratu. Dagan, worshipped at Mari on the Euphrates. Ninurta, confused with
Ningirsu, himself a field god (his symbol is the plough), who
became a battle god. Associate: Gula, goddess of health.
Finally Tammuz, the Dumuzi Abzu, "faithful (or legitimate)
son of Apsu", eclipsed by the previously mentioned gods, his
cult nevertheless persists in popular memory and finally
spread to the west.

The gods were divided into two main categories, the Igigi
or sky gods, and the Anunnaki, or gods living on the earth,
in the waters and the infernal regions. The descriptions of
gods (or demons) in the texts tally with their images on the
monuments; the rules for their representation are fixed and
form a true religious inconography.

The foregoing list may seem long; nevertheless it is quite a
short summary of the Babylonian pantheon. The uncertainty
of the traditions concerning the goddesses attached as associ-
ates to the gods will have been noticed, but more often than not,
these goddesses, like many other gods besides, are merely one
of the aspects of the same deity; the apparent multiplicity is
frequently reflected in a multiplicity of expressions. But even
considering this, the Babylonian religion has an overloaded
pantheon corresponding to the number of cities the gods of
which had to be incorporated; we have seen the same thing
with the thousand gods of the Hittites; we must allow also
for the constant dissipation of divine nature into many forms
which went on through the centuries in the most ancient
religions, as for example with the Egyptians.

MYTHS

The myths represent what the priests thought could be use-
fully told the mass of believers to satisfy their curiosity. They
have not all come down to us, but of those which do still
exist, several are concerned with explaining the reasons for
the death of mankind, as opposed to the immortality of the
gods. The poem of Gilgamesh gives the story of the mighty

deeds of an ancient king of Uruk, who was nevertheless something of a god as his mother was a goddess; with the help of
a companion, Enkidu, he accomplishes deeds worthy of Her-
cules. But the death of his companion strikes terror into him.
He goes on a long voyage to find the only immortal couple,
who survived the flood, and ask their secret. Since the pair had
escaped the cataclysm, the gods, no doubt wishing to show
mercy, established them personally at the ends of the earth and
granted them immortality. The privileged pair reveal to Gilgamesh the existence of a plant which grows at the bottom of
the waters and confers youth. Gilgamesh takes it and rejoices
to carry it home to Uruk; on his return journey, a serpent
steals the plant from him, while he is not watching: a setback
for which man alone is responsible.

Other attempts: Etana, legendary king of Kish, resolved to
go to the god Anu and to beg immortality from him too. An
eagle took him up; but on the way Etana lost heart and let
himself fall to earth. Yet another setback for which the gods
are not responsible.

Lastly, Adapa, summoned by Anu to his court "for having
broken the wings of the South Wind", pleases the god who
offers him the food of life. Being badly advised and suspecting
a trap, he refuses; so humanity goes on dying, still through the
fault of those who could have saved it.

However the gods do possess both water and food of life;
perhaps they need them themselves when they grow old; they
certainly used them to raise the goddess Ishtar back to life
after she had been so unwise as to provoke her sister, queen
of the underworld, and been killed by the gods of the "country
of no return" with their mortal glance, like the Gorgon's, of
later times.

THE CHARACTER OF THE GODS

Being conceived rigidly in the image of men, the gods have
a life based on theirs and have their qualities and defects. In
representation they are distinguished by their dress, the robe

with the woollen drapes, an imitation of animal fleeces, called *kaunakes* by the Greeks; on their heads they wear a tiara encircled with bull's horns, symbolic of their power. When their primitive headdress became more complicated it included leafy branches. After the third dynasty of Ur, they often wear the single robe edged with braid and a turban the outside of which is (or imitates) a lamb-fleece. They frequently hold in one hand a rod and circle, about the meaning of which discussion still continues, or a small vase. The gods are normally accompanied by an attribute which is useful for identification. This attribute can be explained either as an animal that the god has subdued or, contrariwise, has been faithful to him and helped him in his battles, or else as a symbol of his qualities. Oriental taste for analogy led to the choice of attributes suggesting the gods' qualities: the spade for Marduk, the plough for Ningirsu, the bull, the he-goat and, in the late period, the lion-headed eagle holding animals for the gods of fertility and fecundity, who also bear branches, at least in the Jemdet Nasr period. But these attributes give no indication of the memory of any animal-god turning into man. From the very first nothing distinguishes them from man in the earliest representations; later on, the horned tiara and emblems make their appearance and suffice to represent them, especially when there is no room for a complete picture.

As to morals, the gods, as in the Sumerian period, have the human qualities, especially the physical ones, to an extreme degree; they are strong, valiant, like the storm and tempest; their wrath is terrible. They are also good, just and merciful; with time this likeable side of their nature becomes more and more apparent. But their faults are legion and show many signs of their being conceived in a society still in a state of formation and badly controlled; they are vindictive, jealous and gluttonous; they are described as having met for a banquet to make resolutions when they are made tipsy with wine. When the good Utanapishtim, who has survived the flood, offers them a sacrifice, the gods, attracted by the smell, gather like flies around the sacrificer. They may be ignorant of events: Enlil,

who commanded the flood, knows that a man has survived
because he arrives, quite by accident, at the place of sacrifice.
He accuses the other gods of having helped him to escape;
the latter shamelessly lay the blame on Ea who, without any
attempt at honesty, only admits to warning him in a dream,
when he had really given him good warning. When the gods
accorded the first place to Marduk (creation Poem) he suspects
his peers and demands a miracle to prove their sincerity. In
their rage they bite their fingers and strike their thighs; cow-
ardly, and frightened of the flood, they cower under the walls
of their heavenly city and, out of terror, yelp like dogs. They
are primitive, with primitive instincts.

Their powers are rigidly apportioned; even the supreme god
could not interfere outside his sphere. Each one of the gods
refuses to pull up the spirit of the companion of Gilgamesh
without reference to the god of the Underworld. This shows
up a curious aspect of the gods. It appears that their qualities
and powers are not intrinsic to them but linked with their
vesture of divinity, according to the expression in the texts.
In order to become the first among the gods, Marduk finds
himself granted by his peers all their special powers, either by
acclamation or by being given all their weapons. Ishtar in the
Underworld seems not to have been vulnerable before being
stripped of clothing and jewels having some talismanic value.

Furthermore, the gods seem to exercise their power by
means of incantations; in order to punish for boldness a mes-
senger from the gods of the sky, the goddess of the Underworld
smites him with a "mighty curse".

The priests of the first dynasty of Babylon were aware of all
these contradictions and tried to do away with them; the
plethora of deities in the pantheon was real and very obvious.
It was due to the adoption of Sumerian gods who might be
invoked under their Sumerian or Semitic names and to the fact
that many of these gods were but simple aspects of great primitive deities. Texts of the period try to reduce the gods to unity;
we learn that the god Marduk is Ninurta, Nergal, Enlil, Sin,
Shamash, Adad, as well as the god of strength, war, royalty,

illuminator of the darkness, god of justice and rain, and all this so as to put one god at the head of the others, without thought of suppressing them. Then the great gods were grouped into families, mainly sets of three; when the Sumerians had made several successive creations of divine couples, they had already shown the desire to formulate and regulate the material. Finally, bonds of sonship were imposed on the gods. It will be noticed that the sun god is the son of the moon god, as is suitable for caravan drivers who appreciate travelling under protection of the moonlight (*sub amica luna*).

But not all could be lumped together; the gods of the great Sumerian metropolises had to be respected and left some kind of autonomy. The oriental mind could be content with less exactitude than ours and so incongruities which we notice today still persisted.

Among the contradictions which abound in Babylonian religion is the axiom of the immortality of the gods, belied, as we have seen, by the presence from Sumerian times of gods who died, at least temporarily; or at least suffer periods of eclipse; these are the fertility gods, truly Asianic, who sleep through the winter, Tammuz and Gizzida, among others.

The tradition was preserved among the Babylonians. We may see in their poem of the Creation that death did not spare Kingu and Tiamat, both primitive deities; the concept of the gods' immortality was not always absolute; it seems to appear in slow stages, as the divine generations become less and less imperfect. The death of the goddess Ishtar in the Underworld is all that remains of an extremely ancient prototype poem, which was the source of the one called the Descent of Ishtar into the Underworld. The Babylonian recension and a more ancient Sumerian one do not give the reason why Ishtar went to provoke her sister, for there is no suggestion of looking for Dumuzi, and furthermore, Ishtar only comes out of the "land of no return" through the intervention of her fellow deities. As in the case of the Hittite Telepinu, the absence of the goddess was marked by a cessation of earthly life, which alarmed the gods.

CHAPTER X

THE GODS AND MAN

THE GODS AND THE WORLD

The contradictions to be found in the nature of the gods are seen also in their relations with the universe; they are the masters, and rule it according to laws which they ratify every year in an assembly, when they meet to settle the fates. But, afterwards, whether or not they can intervene and alter them is not certain, for fate must exist or not, and if it does, the gods have set a limit to their own power. First of all, the world had to be created, and here we are faced with several traditions. The Sumerians of Nippur left this one: Anu, actually "father of the gods", creates the Anunnaki, a term meaning the "great gods"; everything else is left undone, there are no domestic animals and the use of cereals is quite unknown. The Anunnaki create all such things and men are able to thrive.

In a poem called the Chaldean Cosmogony, the question of origins is dealt with: all the land was sea. The holy cities, like Eridu, emerge from it, then Babylon with its temple and its god Marduk; he weaves a hurdle which he places on the water, creates some earth to cover the hurdle and, to live on the earth, men, whom he makes from his union with the goddess Aruru, then grass and trees, and domestic animals. After this, Nippur and Uruk appear. The position of priority given to Eridu and Babylon is due to the cosmogony being invented by the priests of Eridu and Babylon, and therefore quite late. Another tale gives the following short account of creation in slow stages: Anu creates the day, from this comes the earth, from the earth come rivers, from these the creative mud channels which produce the worm, and all this to obtain an incantation against the tooth-ache worm! It fell to the first dynasty of Babylon to give definitive form to these diverse foundations, and the result, composed to the glory of the national god Marduk, lasted until the end of Mesopotamian history; a summary account appears below.

In Assyria, beliefs were identical, but, following the example of Babylon, Assyria chose a state god in the person of Assur, whose name merely replaces that of Marduk in all the actions ascribed to that god. This creation of a state god superior to the others might have led to monotheism. Nothing of the sort, in fact, happened; a hierarchy was formed but there was no expulsion from the pantheon. Religion could recommend trust in one god as opposed to others, but it could not deny their existence.

The classic text is the poem of Creation, known as *Enuma elish* ("When on high") from its first two words. The text begins by stating that there was nothing, for "on high, the sky was not named, below the earth had received no name . . . nor was any name named". All is in confusion: Apsu, the fresh water, and Tiamat, the sea. We know that the gods are born in pairs for the world on high and for the world below; among the first Anu is born whose son, Ea, kills Apsu to put an end to his plots and becomes king of his domains. But Tiamat longs for vengeance; with the help of a god, Kingu, to whom she delivers the tablets of fate, she prepares for the battle. Ea and Anu refuse to fight, so Marduk, son of Ea, offers to do so provided the control of the fates is given into his hands. A banquet is held at which the gods eat and drink deep and they bestow their powers on Marduk. He has doubts, as we have mentioned, and asks for a sign; so the gods bring a garment before him which he can cause to disappear and reappear at will. The proof is conclusive and Marduk goes to fight. Tiamat, a fearsome dragon, opens an enormous mouth, Marduk flings the four Winds, his allies, into it and transfixes the by now breathless Tiamat. Kingu is captured. Marduk stands on the carcase of Tiamat, vaunts his victory, and splits the body in two "like an oyster"; he makes the earth from one half; in the other, he founds a palace for the gods in the sky.

The Mesopotamian conception of the world is still obscure. The earth, a flat surface, rested on the void of fresh waters, encircled by sea. From the edges of this surface, the heavenly hemisphere with its stars rose like a dish cover, and above was the domain of the gods.

The *Enuma elish* poem also lists the titles granted to Marduk after his victory, and this gives a good example of the power of "name". The gods vie with each other in finding epithets for him, at first sight merely adulatory, but which in fact carry with them the powers they refer to. The "fifty names" of Marduk may be compared with the "ninety-nine beautiful names" of Allah. This part of the poem is an insertion having a political aim, being made by the priests of Babylon in their desire to grant the highest position to their own state god.

THE GODS AND MAN

It remained for man to be created. For this purpose, Marduk has the powers of Ea, one of whose names is the "potter god", in imitation of the Egyptian god Knum who models figurines like the potter, and gives them life with his own breath. Ea, through the art of Marduk, does the same and mixes in the blood of Kingu, by now executed. Man, therefore, has something divine in him; but Kingu was a rebel god; can this be why mankind so troubles the gods? This poem and other traditions state expressly the purpose for which man was created; to worship the gods and so to acquit them from having to trouble about anything. This was the religious charter of the Mesopotamians who lived in fear of the gods; but there was the added duty for man to "bring to fullness all that was lacking, and to answer for the swelling of Creation" (British Museum text), as was remarked by Bottero, to whom we owe a most penetrating study of Babylonian religion. This greatly enlarges the scope of human duties and legislators are careful to emphasize the fact that they have fulfilled the obligations imposed on them by these conditions. Hammurabi, in his Code of Laws, states that he was raised up to "make justice shine forth, to prevent the powerful from wronging the weak". It is in the light of this precept that we should judge the collections of laws which have come down to us. In the examination of his sins, the repentant believer must give equal consideration to crimes against the laws and against the gods, for the laws are inspired by the divine will.

This is evident from all the laws of western Asia that have been found, and the spirit of the early ones still inspires the later. The innovations of the Sumerian reformer Urukagina nevertheless vary in value; he is careful to protect the weak; but when he boasts of having left no survivor in the north or south of Sumer, one may well remain in doubt as to the true nature of his changes.

The Babylonian was by no means unimpressed by the hardness of life, the troubles and evils that befall man for which he sees no reason except the existence of an evil divinity, or one that he has annoyed. The first idea must be excluded; the gods are terrible and powerful, but just, as man must recognize; little by little he grants that they are merciful. He must, therefore, have annoyed the god by breaking his laws, either religious (lack of devotion) or civil, for civil laws derive from religion in the last analysis. In both cases, there is more than mere fault, there is sin, and the wrathful god has "turned away" his face from the believer. If the matter is serious, the god himself can inflict the punishments of the loss of goods, family sorrows, or loss of health.

In most cases the punishment is indirect; it is applied by one of the demons populating the universe whose importance cannot be over stressed. Who are these demons? Some are by nature partly divine but inferior; they are the "bile" of the gods; they are naturally evil, often classified in groups of seven; they haunt the streets at night, they lie in wait for the lone traveller, and during the day are shut up in the mountains. Many of them bear a name indicating their speciality; some of the most important are called Namtaru, identified with the plague, for they cause most of the illnesses of man and beast. They upset the order of things, cause misunderstanding in families, destroy, steal and, when not terrible, are at least insufferable, making rest impossible with their uproar. But there is another class of demons deriving from mankind, ghosts, spectres, unsatisfied avengers, the spirits of those who have not attained what they wished in life or what they hoped for in death: the man killed in the desert, doomed, killed accidentally, the woman dead unmarried, the dead man who receives no funerary offerings. This crowd of demons grows endlessly, enlarged by the imagination of men needing to find something or someone responsible for the evils which befall them.

The desert, for us an empty space, for the Mesopotamians was populated, even to excess, with demons. The underworld expanded and contracted with the seasons. When the drought came and the steppe was burnt, the domain of Ishtar diminished in proportion and Dumuzi transformed himself during this period, being the antagonist of the goddess and her beneficent behaviour. In her laments, she wept for the change and the presence of evil spirits in her usual kingdom. It is wrong, therefore, to speak of fertility gods dying; they have a period of inactivity which is to the advantage of their adversaries. The poem of the Descent of Ishtar into Hell gives no reason for the adventure. It must be something to do with the goddess's yearly urge for this war, in Ishtar's hate for her sister, which made her unable to refrain from attacking the Queen of the Underworld on sight.

But there were cases in which the believer thought that he was in the right regarding the deity afflicting him. A poem called "The Righteous Sufferer", at one time well known, gave sad expression to the position. The Righteous Man, or at least the man who thinks himself so, examines his conscience: he has been good towards his neighbour and has rendered due worship to the gods. Here a doubt enters: can it be that our idea of what is good strikes the gods as evil? He is stricken in health, he loses his goods and his friends abandon him. Now, Babylonian religion had, properly speaking, no such notion as that of a test and all this would appear to form part of a divine order whereby the state god of the first dynasty of Babylon might be glorified. Marduk, who had nothing to do with the sufferings of the Righteous Man, takes pity on him and restores him to his friends, health and goods. Glory be to Marduk!

The demons have been the object of many representations. Both good and bad are shown as hybrids, half beast, half man. The great winged bulls in the Louvre, good spirits which guarded the entrance to the palace of King Sargon II of Assyria, are calm and majestic. The bad demons appear grinning evilly and threatening. Their images used to be carried on the body as a protection against what they represented. In fact, once they were known and named, which was accomplished by inscribing their name, they were made incapable of doing harm.

One of these amulets is the image of Lamashtu, a demoness, thought to be the daughter of Anu, who made pregnant women her victims or took charge of the newborn child. The charms suitable to counteract her influence are also known to us; but it must not be forgotten that demons only specialized as an addition to their normal activities and might cause harm in any circumstances, whence their generic name of "the Seven" or even "the Seven times Seven". They were conjured in the name of the sky and the earth, or of one god in particular. They were threatened, but promises were also made to them to persuade them to give way; these promises were to pay tribute of jewellery, provisions for their journeys and especially of another resting place. Here we find the idea of a substitute; it may be a piglet or a lamb that the exorcist declared to be ill, or even a mere reed. At all events, these promises are all a little in the nature of a decoy. In the Clercq collection there is a bronze exorcism plaque which shows the objects offered to Lamashtu to make her go away. The substitute idea went even further; in order to safeguard the king's person (he was the high priest) who might be threatened by evil chance, a temporary substitute was nominated to take the risks for him.

We have mentioned that punishment could be applied directly by the gods. This is the subject of a poem about "the

Flood", which was supposed to wipe out mankind, considered evil enough by the gods to deserve total destruction. The god Ea, represented in the texts as a kindly god, determined to restrict the disaster; indirectly, out of fear of his fellows, he warned the man whom he wished to save by bringing him as close as he could to his dwelling and whispering his warning through a flimsy wall. The faithful man therefore made his preparations, putting all his family and all kinds of animals into a boat. The text describes in words of savage majesty the unleashing of the storm, the waves subsiding and the ship going aground on a mountain, with the story, as in the Bible, of birds being released and coming back until the dry land appeared. Then the just man came out of his ark and made a sacrifice; we already know how the gods received it and how the quarrel arose between Enlil and Ea. In the end, the gods placed the protégé with his wife in a distant corner of the world, and the pair were granted immortality.

Excavations have revealed signs of a flood in several places and there has been considerable discussion about these discoveries at Ur and Kish; there are indeed deposits, but of different periods, of very limited extent, and due to floods caused by ordinary overflowing but of abnormal volume, as happened from time to time.

This is the only citable example of a case of immortality and the Mesopotamians, faced with the inevitability of death, explained it away as due to human error, as we have seen.

CHAPTER XI

WORSHIP AND RELIGIOUS PRACTICES

WORSHIP

Man's homage to the gods was rendered in the temples; many remains of these have been found in digs, sometimes detached and sometimes joined to a palace. The usual form, after the attainment of power by the Semites, is of a court with an altar for sacrifice, opposite the entrance of the temple which had a large hall before the cella containing the statue of the god, sometimes itself preceded by an antecella.

Benches were provided for the offerings brought and for statues put up *ex voto* by the faithful. Near the temple was the storeyed tower, or ziggurat. Two types are known of these towers. In one, the tower was made of terraces piled on top of one another with a ramp going from one to the next up to the top, where there was a small temple for the god to enter if he so wished. The other consisted of less regular terraces. The lowest were mounted by ramps or exterior staircases, the others by little staircases from one storey to the next. These towers, prototypes of the tower of Babel, are found all over Mesopotamia and, from the evidence provided by the digs, are comparable only in shape with the Egyptian pyramid concealing a royal tomb, for the ziggurat covers nothing at all. For the first type we may cite the first ever studied, at Khorsabad, near Ninive, for the second type, the one at Ur. The latest discovery, still being cleared, is the one of Choga Zanbil near Susa, and is of a different model from that of Mesopotamia.

The most famous temple in Babylonia was the Esagil at Babylon. With its dependencies it covered an area of nearly sixty acres (little remains of the temple itself), including its ziggurat the Etemenanki, "foundation temple of sky and earth".

This idea of communication between the heavenly and earthly worlds is seen in some of their names (e.g. "link between sky and earth") and shows the religious significance of these buildings. But it is also possible that according to a popular tradition they were cenotaphs of divinity, symbolic of the fertility principle and subject to annual eclipse. When Herodotus visited Babylon he was told that the ziggurat was the "tomb of the god Bel". Moreover, these monuments served as observatories for the priests to make predictions from the stars. Temple, ziggurat, priests' lodgings and warehouses were all built in one great enclosure.

Here we must recall what has been said about "name" and the value attached to it; any ziggurat or temple has a name, which is a statement of what it really is. Any statue (always destined for the temple) is marked with the name of the believer offering it; this name, like that of the statue, states a quality and proclaims the god's good care of his subject. The words of the motto take on real existence for the Babylonian. The same applies to *ex votos* and instruments used in worship, enfolding the whole in an atmosphere of sacredness in which all combines to exalt the power of the god and to provoke (as the expression has it) his good-will.

A large number of priests was attached to the temple under a High Priest who was the king (who delegated his powers and whose presence is only required in certain circumstances). The king was not a god as in Egypt, but his representative; he was said to be named by the gods the husband of some goddess or other, or fed on her milk in his infancy. The deification of kings was rare, and the regular offerings sometimes seen at their statues were offerings which these statues, living since they had a name, should pass on to the gods. Because of the high value attached to the king's person, religion devised a system whereby, whenever he was threatened by an evil presage, a substitute should run the risks in his place.

The priests were divided into administrators, celebrants, sacrificers, diviners and exorcists, cantors and musicians. We possess the ritual of the "lamenter" (*kalu*) whose object was to soften the hearts of the gods. The temple also had priestesses with a superior at their head; they included hierodules, sacred prostitutes, whose actions by virtue of the interdependence of sky and earth, were supposed to provoke the sacred marriage of the gods in the sky, the source of fertility on earth. The priests took a share of the offerings and, under the first dynasty of Babylon and the Seleucids, it was common to see the best endowed of them trading in these revenues, by notarial deed. The temple also sheltered janitors, cooks and barbers, for it was an independent living-unit and lent out grain and haulage animals from its enormous income. The accounts, the reception and employment of offerings, were all done by the scribes, who often had a school attached to the temple; they were the repository of all knowledge, sacred and profane.

Every day the divine statue was washed, perfumed and dressed as a living being; the priests offered it gargantuan meals in dishes of gold and silver, and divided up what remained among themselves. Offerings and sacrifices, which were overwhelmingly of food, made up the bulk of these meals; but certain offerings, like libations, the pouring out of milk, wine, oil or even water, before the god were intended to bring about divine beneficence in the shape of rain, overflowing of the rivers and other sources of wealth. The whole cult was rigorously ordered; we possess the New Year Ritual and it is of extreme complexity; the slightest fault in the ceremony made it useless; so for the eve of a great feast a service of expiation was devised for the faults that would certainly be committed the next day.

DIVINATION AND MAGIC

These two practices, regarded by the Babylonians as essentially religious, were the special function of certain priests. For instance, divination was practised by the *baru* ("inspector") and concerned the sun-god Shamash. It was thought the gods, having fixed men's destiny, showed it or gave indications of what it would be by means of signs to be seen in material things, for there was complete interrelation of sky and earth.

There were numberless means of divination and everything could be used as matter for giving portent. Firstly, the revelations made by the gods to the faithful in sleep, since for the Babylonian dreams possess real value and true existence; all that is imagined can and must be explained; attention must be paid to every act in life and everything met with; all things have meaning and often on different levels. At the same time one must beware of what is forbidden, for there are favourable days and unlucky ones. All the things that can be met with are listed in the collections and some are guaranteed by examples of presages given to the kings of old in various circumstances. Furthermore, divination has a long history, having been revealed, according to tradition, to a king before the flood. But it is a learned matter, not within the reach of lesser folk —extispicy and hepatoscopy, the examination of the entrails and liver of a victim, either sheep or goat. The priests codified the rules and the meaning of any anomaly was fixed.

There are even clay models of livers showing all possible malformations of the organ. This form of divination is found in Etruria, as is that made from observing the flight of birds favoured by the Hittites. Astrology too had its vogue, but it was incomplete, for the procession of the equinoxes was unknown. Determination of astral positions at birth, as was later practised, was impossible. Babylonian astrology, except at a very late period, was restricted to meteorological consultations. Books of divination, like those dealing with magic, constitute an important part of the Babylonian and Assyrian literature that has come down to us.

Magic, too, is allowable when practised by priests; its purpose is to exorcize the demons which possess individuals when they have earned the wrath of the gods or have suffered from the ill-deeds of sorcerers (the latter being punished by death if discovered). The priests for exorcism are the *ashipu*, who pronounce the incantation, and the *mahmashu*, dressed in red, the anti-demoniac colour. They receive their powers from Marduk who received them himself from his father Ea. It must first be established what has angered the god. The list of inquiries to be made is fixed and long, for the believer may have committed any number of voluntary faults, against his neighbour, against society which is protected, so say the law-givers, by laws made under the god's protection, and against the gods themselves, "spitting" in the river, for example. The river is god and to entrust a child to it is not to abandon it but to put it under august protection. The believer may have been in contact, even at a distance, through a tool or garment, with someone under the influence of a sorcerer or with a contaminated being. The lists, in this form: "Has he done this, or that?" are therefore long; in the course of time they received additions and show repetitions. But no matter, it is enough for the sin, even unconscious, to be pronounced (it is now known, for it has been "named"); the same for the demon who has brought about the possessing and the lists are consulted for this. After this, the exorcism; the priests recite the strictly established formulas and conjure the demons in the name of the great gods who cannot avoid responding to a correctly pronounced exorcism. This belief justified the value attached to cursing. If done according to rule, in the name of this power, or that, the god concerned could not help interfering. In the poem of Gilgamesh, Enkidu, his friend, curses the hierodule who initiated him to civilization. The god Shamash reproves him for his injustice; he nevertheless complies by metamorphizing the hierodule into a bitch.

All this is accompanied by libations and incensing. The sinner becomes once more the "son of his god" and the demon must seek another victim. At times, precautions are multiplied; woollen knots, symbols of the possession, are untied or burnt, a statuette of the sorcerer is burnt, the classic hoodoo procedure; sometimes a pact will be made with the demon; a sacrificial victim is assimilated to the sinner by means of a ritual and becomes his substitute, the demon falling into the trap made for him. If the texts are examined it will be seen that magic does not claim to do more than exorcize the possessed; invisibility and transformations are not within its scope and are restricted to the gods.

MEDICINE

This is nothing but an application of divination, especially of magic, and as such deserves to be treated as part of religion. Medical instruction did exist in Babylonia, in spite of what Herodotus said, and, for us, it has two aspects: at first, medicine was priestly: in the late period, it did try to make use of observation. In the first period, the sick man is only a sinner, prey to the demons. There are doctors (*azu*) to heal him but their practices are more or less those of the priests and this is what happens: in order to know where the illness that afflicts him comes from, the priest doctor refers to the list of sins, unless the complaint be so commonplace as to have been catalogued long before (for instance, drunkenness considered as poisoning). Once the fault is named, with the name of the tormentor, the simple fact of having mentioned them means that the conjuration will deliver the sick man from it, whether or not he is provided with a substitute (sometimes merely a reed his own height) ritually declared to be the patient. Then it is a matter of keeping him in health; this is done by performing works for the temple and carrying amulets and talismans. In order to unite the priests' efforts with his own, the doctor administers drugs as nauseous as possible to the patient so as to make the demon want to move out. In the second period, under the Sargonids, these medicines are no longer in use and the field of exorcism is restricted; the symptoms of various illnesses are known and there are real formulas of remedies, always composed of many medicines in doses more often than not impossible to take, which suggests that the identification of some of them is surely wrong. Prognosis is no longer based on portents (before, a doctor going to see a patient used to note them while still on his way), but on exact observation; the notion of the critical period is known, foreshadowing Hippocrates. The doctor names the diseases; if the patient is ill he is said to be afflicted with *amuriqanu*. This word merely means "being yellow", but we should not laugh; in a similar case, we call it "jaundice". A bronze plaquette in the Clercq collection, which was thought before to be a scene in hell, is really an important medical consultation with the patient lying down and the exorcists dressed in a costume like the body of a fish (a sign of the god Ea), and good and evil spirits.

Some remarks should be made on the ritual of divination and magic. The interdependence of sky and earth applies to the sky in the extension of symbolism on all levels of existence to the divine beings; i.e. one god is symbolized by a star, a number, a stone, a vegetable, metal, a cloth and a colour; he is the patron of certain trades. Modern astrology states this absolutely. Babylonian predictions have been repeated throughout the ages; Cicero in his divination, Artemidorus of Daldia and our own keys to dreams all reproduce Babylonian interpretations. Nor has magical procedure changed; the magic ring, circles and hoodoo figurines are all the same. Whereas the world is in a state of perpetual and rapid change, two techniques, divination and magic, have been able to stay unchanged for several thousands of years.

Having given these examples of ritual, we must say something about the great feasts of Babylon; the best known is the feast of the Akitu, held in the month of Nisan, the first month of the year which began in spring. Here is what happened: it lasted several days. First of all, the gods of the provinces (their statues) arrive at the capital and go to do homage to Marduk at the Esagil temple; then comes the procession. Marduk, invited by the king, is standing in his chariot; he joins the "Way of Processions", the walls of which are covered with varnished bricks, adorned with symbolic animals on blue background. The procession goes through the gate of Ishtar, stops at the river's edge where Marduk takes his boat (we must not forget that the gods have a self-contained household); the boat goes up the river a little, and then the procession moves across country and goes to the temple of the New Year. There the *Enuma elish* is solemnly read, recalling Marduk's battle with Tiamat; it may have been mimed; once more Marduk is glorified by his peers. After the return to Babylon, the god and goddess are put into the marriage chamber for the sacred marriage which is to spread fertility and fecundity in Babylonia. It is conjectured that at this point the king, or High Priest, and the High Priestess substituted themselves for the statues for the rite to be properly carried out. After fixing the annual destinies of Babylon, the gods go back to their provincial temples. This feast is a perfect example of the fusion of the Semitic contribution: Marduk's fight, the creation of the world, the pre-eminence of Babylon, and of the Sumerian naturistic religion represented by the final hierogamy.

THE NEXT WORLD

The above is an account of the Babylonian's relations with the world of the heavens; let us now see his relations with the underworld, Hell, known to him as "the great land, the country of no return". In the beginning, Ishtar's sister, Ereshkigal, ruled this domain. A myth tells us that the god Nergal had no wife and was looking for a kingdom; he offended the goddess who asked the gods to deliver him to her to be put to death. Nergal, joined by a few demons, took the offensive, passed the seven doors of Hell, fell upon Ereshkigal and raised his sword to cut off her head. Without hesitating, Ereshkigal offered to be his wife and share her royal status. So it came about and, aided by the Igigi, rather vague gods of Hell, the pair ruled over the shades. They were fearful to behold, but if Nergal did sometimes make incursions on to the earth to go recruiting, bearing plague, famine or some other scourge, the two deities exercised no cruelty over their subjects. The life they led below was itself enough to make their stay difficult and fearsome. The dead depicted in some texts as covered with "garments of wings", have a slow, miserable life. All is dark, and dust, that scourge of the Orient, is everywhere. The dead must provide for their sustenance; without any funeral offerings, they must needs have recourse to the left-overs of the living, rubbish thrown out on the streets. Such, at any rate, is the painful picture given by the spirit of Enkidu, the friend of Gilgamesh, who was granted the special favour of returning to the earth for a few moments to describe to him his sad state. If, on the one hand, the dead have no food, on the other Enkidu describes those fallen in battle, helped and refreshed by their friends. But such exceptions are rare, and the sad life of the dead follows but logically the existence of every day, in which the Babylonian, hemmed in by taboos and fatal portents, led a life without hope.

THE VALUE OF THE MESOPOTAMIAN RELIGION

The religion of Sumer, afterwards of Babylon, is, thanks to its monuments, the most ancient of ancient western Asia that we can know well; it takes us about fifty centuries into the past. It is an Asianic type of religion, that is, worshipping the principles of fertility and fecundity, like the older, neighbouring religions of the Hittites, Hurrites, Urartu, Elam and Phoenicia.

Under the influence of contacts with the Semites of the land of Akkad, north of Sumer, at the beginning of history, Sumerian religion received their imprint, which, however, was still not enough for the religion of the Babylonians and Assyrians, which developed from it, to be called Semitic. It is possible to be struck by formal likenesses between the two religions, but Babylonian religion is nothing more than a remaking of Sumerian, itself essentially naturistic.

It is impossible that Sumero-Babylonian religion should not have evolved during its existence of 3000 years and, in fact, the list of sins which the believer may commit, though in complete disorder, enumerates some, alongside those committed against the rules of ritual, which we today consider as such together with sins against society, thereby showing a developed spirit that no longer corresponds to the picture of the gods presented by primitive religion.

This progress is partly due to the achievements of Babylonian civilization, but also to the efforts to unify beliefs made by the priests of Babylon. The uncertainty and contradiction which remain are doubtless the result of respect for the traditions of old and venerated cities, which no one dared to abolish, and also to the satisfaction of oriental minds with exactness less strict than we should require in the west.

Though starting from such weak grounds, Babylonian religion, reformed in this way, was nevertheless able to shed some honour on its devotees. But its inveterate polytheism and belief in the inevitable malefice of demons, resulted in the most depressing superstition, without any hope of a better world hereafter. The possibility of future retribution, just perceptible in the last days of its history, was never clearly formulated. The Egyptian ideal of the next world, though depreciated by the tricks allowed to believers at the judgement, was totally lacking in Babylon, and this allows us, I believe, to consider its religion as one of the gloomiest that ever existed.

PART III

IRANIAN RELIGION
by J. Duchesne-Guillemin

INTRODUCTION

After Iran had yielded to Islam, the ancient religion survived in a mountain district, at Yezd, and among the Parsis of Bombay, the descendants of Iranian refugees.

The origins of this religion are tied up with those of the Iranian people, a separate branch of the Indo-European nation. The religion common to the whole of this nation was raised in Iran to a higher level, half way between the mystical Hima-layas and the islands of philosophy. Iran even surpassed its neighbours, India and Greece, or preceded them, in declaring for monotheism, no doubt owing to the strong personality of Zarathushtra (Zoroaster), with whom we can only compare the prophets of Israel. It was especially the dualism, the opposition of the demon Ahriman to the god Ormazd, which struck the Greeks, like the customs of the Magians and sciences, astral and otherwise, rightly or wrongly attributed to them. The mysteries of Mithra were known to be of Iranian origin. Mani-cheism which, with Mithraism, was the great rival of early Christianity, was only a variation, though certainly hardly orthodox, of Iranian religion.

Antiquity came to look upon Zoroaster and the more or less authentic Magians as the forerunners and guarantors of its own wisdom, both pagan and Christian. Zoroaster was believed to have taught Pythagoras; philosophy, astrology, alchemy, theurgy, magic, etc., were all reflected as it were in a mirror in the so-called Chaldean doctrines, the bulk of the writings ascribed to the wise men being only apocryphal; a tremendous projection of Greek concepts mingled with a smattering of Iranian ideas.

For Christians, Iran was always above all the land of the three Magi who, guided by a star, came to worship at Bethle-hem. Further, continuing Jewish tradition, they identified

Zoroaster with Ezechiel, Nemrod, Seth, Balaam, Baruch, and even, through the last mentioned, with Christ himself. After Justinian, Zoroaster and the Magians could be quoted by apologists as belonging to the witnesses from outside that they invoked to establish and justify the truth of Christianity in pagan eyes.

On the other hand, Zoroaster was the founder of a particularly abominable superstition: astrology and Chaldean magic. For instance, in the pseudo-Clementine Recognitions, he figures as an arch-heretic. What is more, Iran was also the land of the Manicheans and was therefore at the bottom of Catharism, that major heresy of the Middle Ages. Catharism was constantly identified by the defenders of orthodoxy with the religion of Mani. It appears to us now as a form of gnosticism without any special connexion with Manicheism, but the first heresiologists of the eleventh century—at least those who, like Ademar of Chabannes, had some culture, turned naturally to the Fathers of the Church and their anti-Manichean polemic the better to understand and combat the heretics of their own time.

The religious history of Iran has therefore never ceased to interest western scholars, especially for the light on their own past they hoped to gain from it; unfortunately, it is difficult to write. The sources, whether native documents or Greek, Armenian or Arabic evidence, etc., are few, spread out through the centuries in time and often demand great labour for their interpretation. Their study demands such hard apprenticeship that no Iranist may boast of having set himself to study them all: an inevitable diversity in the manner of preparation of each shows up the variety of temperaments, and makes for a rather picturesque intellectual family. As no member agrees with another on hardly anything, any attempt at popularization made by one cannot fail to be censured by another: one has even gone so far as to write that the only honest way to make the Gathas of Zarathushtra known to the public was to present them to it in the original, of which, without spending ten years at them alone, it would understand not a word.

No claim is made below to proceed from the facts to their interpretation—more space would have been required. But, here and there, texts have been quoted, in a good translation; in order to fix the ideas, points and problems have been grouped under a series of headings, as definitions of terms. Relations with Greece, Israel and gnosticism have been left to the end.

CHAPTER XII

A SHORT GLOSSARY OF
IRANIAN RELIGION

IRAN

Shortened from Iran-shahr, "Land of the Aryas". The language and civilization of Iran, before Islam, were related to those of Aryan India. A comparison of Iranian texts (Avesta, see below) and Indian ones (Veda, etc.) enables us to reconstitute the religion of the Indo-Iranians (or Aryas) before this branch of the Indo-European nation split into two groups, one of which invaded India, the other Iran.

The territory conquered by the Iranians included, apart from present-day Iran, Baluchistan, Afghanistan, Russian Turkestan as far as the Syr-darya (Jaxartes), the Aral and Caspian seas, and part of southern Russia as far as the shores of the Black Sea. Dialectally this territory was divided into four main regions, each of which played its own part in the history of the whole nation. The east, separated from the west by the great central desert of the Iranian plateau, except for the series of oases south of the Caspian, was the scene of the birth and first expansion of Zoroastrian religion. The north-west, that is, the south of the Caspian and the Caucasus, was the country of the Medes, whose king Deioces founded the first Iranian empire (Herodotus, I, 96). The south-west, lying along the Persian Gulf, was the land of the Persae, whose dialect was clearly differentiated from the rest. Their king, Cyrus, founded the Achaemenid Empire in the middle of the sixth century B.C., which was to roll back the frontiers of the Mede empire while crushing the Babylonian, threaten Greece and only succumb to Alexander (331). The religion of the Archaemenids is known only summarily from rock inscriptions.

The north was inhabited by nomads, Sacae or Scythians, whose rôle, through their incursions southwards, was largely episodic.

A century and a half after the death of Alexander, the hegemony passed to the Parthians who came from the southeast of the Caspian. This was the Arsacid empire. In 224 A.D., the centre of political power returned to Persia, under the Sassanids, who reigned until the Islamic conquest. Zoroastrianism—the previous history of which is obscure—became the official religion of the Sassanian empire. It had to contend not only with Christianity and Manicheism, but with a very widespread form of astral fatalism, Zervanism or Time religion. Tolerated by the (see below) Muslim conquerors, Zoroastrianism, in spite of numerous conversions to the new order, continued to flourish for several centuries, especially during the ninth. (For the rest of its history, see below, Parseeism.)

MAGIANS

A Mede tribe, according to Herodotus, who described their peculiar customs. They neither buried nor burnt their dead, but exposed them to the birds. They practised consanguineous marriage and were specialists in oneiromancy, astrology and magic (this last art owes its name to them). They had a dualist conception of the world, distinguishing between the animals it was forbidden to kill and those whose slaughter was obligatory.

During the first years of the reign of Darius, when the sovereign himself was conquering Egypt, the Magian Gaumata, making himself out to be Smerdis, Cambyses' brother, of whose death he had heard, seized power. Darius returned, put him and several other Magians to death and resumed control. The event was commemorated each year afterwards by a feast called "The Slaughter of the Magians". But their influence grew steadily in the state and they finally obtained a monopoly over all religion. The religion of the Avesta (see below) is the result of the fusion of the Zoroastrian reform with Magian doctrines and customs, together with popular cults and habits. The Magians made out Zarathushtra as one of themselves so as to pass as the direct heirs of the first converts. In fact, the term *magu*, "Magian", is not attested at all in the *gathas* (see below, Avesta) and only once in the Avesta. But there is in the *gathas* a word, *magavan*, resembling the first, to which, on a final analysis, it may be related. It seems to mean "sharing in the alliance, the mystic gift". The existence of this term undoubtedly made the appropriation of Zoroastrianism easier for the Magians. In the Arsacid period the superiors of the religious hierarchy no longer bore the name of *magupat*, "chief of the Magians", as they did under the Sassanians, and which they retained as *mobed*.

ZARATHUSHTRA

He was known by the surname of Spitama. He was a prophet of ancient Iran, known to the Greeks (from the Platonic dialogue *Alcibiades I* and Xanthos the Lydian, quoted by Nicholas of Damascus) as Zoroaster. According to the Iranian tradition (which there is no reason to doubt) he lived 258 years before Alexander, i.e. 258 years before Alexander's arrival in Iran (330). The principal event of Zarathushtra's life took place, either his first vision, at the age of thirty, or the beginning of his preaching, at forty, or his conversion of King Vishtasp, when he was forty. Vishtasp, who must not be confused (as by the ancients) with his namesake the father of Darius, seems to have reigned over a motley collection of peoples making up what we might call "Greater Khorasmia", stretching from the Aral and the Caspian seas to northern Baluchistan. Tradition makes him the last of a line of kings. It was probably his empire that Cyrus put an end to, just as he had destroyed that of the Medes.

Faced with the failure of his preaching, Zarathushtra had to flee and only later did he gain the protection of Vishtasp. But there is nothing to prove that he came originally from Media. All the traditions which place the birth (and preaching) of Zarathushtra in Media are late and reflect the political situation of the Sassanian period.

Zarathushtra was a minor lordling, owning livestock and retainers and brought up on traditional forms of religion. The society in which he lived was still pastoral and only partly settled on the land. After a revelation, he began to preach the eminent holiness of Ahura Mazda, "the Wise Lord" (see below), the coming of his kingdom in the near future, and the duty of every man to decide in his favour, against the supporters of Mithra, whose cult was bloody and whose life was nomadic. Chased from his home, he set out to look for a protector who would help him to realize his ideals of justice, and he managed to convert King Vishtasp. He found other supporters at the court of the king, notably in one Jamasp, of whom legend records that he married his daughter. He preached a kind of holy war against the enemies of his reform, now identified with the enemies of the power of Vishtasp. After his death, his daughter Puruchista and other believers perpetuated his memory and carried on his work. But the message of the founder cannot have been kept pure and Zoroastrian religion, as reflected in the whole Avesta, is an amalgam containing many old elements opposed by the prophet; sometimes a compromise was found between his preaching and traditional cults and beliefs.

Zarathushtra's preaching is preserved for us in the *gathas*, works of strong feeling, more lyric than didactic, but from which it is possible to extract a doctrine. Zarathushtra protested against bloody sacrifice and that of *haoma*.

Haoma, the juice of a giant plant used for sacrifice, was the equivalent of the Indian soma. By drinking fermented soma, the Vedic sacrificer thought to equal the gods and gain heavenly immortality. He was not only fulfilling a fertility rite, a means of promoting vegetable life, just as bloody sacrifice promoted animal and human life; he sought to transcend life itself, to escape human conditions in an ecstasy of drunkenness. This ritual was connected with the sacrifice of the ox. Zarathushtra repudiated both—while tolerating, perhaps, a non-orgiastic form of the latter. The great, if not the only, means of uniting oneself with God was to unite oneself with his justice, ritually symbolized by fire. This is why Zarathushtra allowed the fire sacrifice to continue, as a symbol of the struggle against the forces of evil.

He substitutes the myth of the complaint of the ox for the one relating the origin of the sacrifice of the ox. The ox asks for protection; this is granted him by the breeder, who looks after him, and by the warrior, who defends him against the attacks of the nomads and sacrificers: all this conforms to the divine order revealed by the prophet. In this way, the social order is settled. At the same time, the figure of Yima who, in the myth, presided over the first sacrifice, is degraded. On the other hand, an original myth is made prominent in the preaching, the myth of the Choice, an expression of systematic dualism containing the play of the whole of human—and divine—destiny.

The whole of Zarathushtra's theology seems to start from the vision in which the holiness and beneficence of Ahura Mazda appeared to him. Equally beneficent is one of two spirits, who, in the old religion, watched over beginnings: Spanta Mainyu. In the very beginning, this spirit chose the good, life, intelligence and light, whereas the other, Ahra Mainyu, "the Destroyer Spirit", chose evil, non-life, stupidity and darkness. In the same way, all the traditional oppositions, conspicuously reflected in old myths—the struggle of the star Tishtrya (Sirius) against the demon of dryness, Apaosha, etc., are combined in a single, universal struggle between two camps. The choice of the two spirits is the model of the choice imposed on every man, sanctioned, after the great test, soon to come, by a retribution. The daevas, former gods (see below, Ahura Mazda) chose badly, putting themselves on the side of evil to ruin men's existence. Nevertheless, man's choice remains free. He must side, "in thought, word and deed", with Ahura Mazda and the

Amasha Spantas (see below), "kindly immortals" who rule the world of good.

Zarathushtra announces that a new world will soon come about, following the great judgement separating the followers of good and of evil. Only the former will share in the second existence, thought of as carried out on earth. But there persists, alongside this eschatological hope, a belief in life after death, on which Zarathushtra still makes the imprint of his dualism. Souls will be judged, individually, at death, and rewarded with life in the Abode of Light, or punished with the pains of a dark and disgusting Hell. The two concepts, of the renewal of the world and the fate of souls after death, were later to be harmonized in one system (see below, Eschatology), which included the individual judgement of souls, then a resurrection of the body followed by final judgement of definite triumph for the good.

AVESTA

The sacred book of the Parsees. The text would fill an octavo volume of 500 pages. This Avesta only represents about one quarter of the former one, of which we possess a summary. The contents of the modern Avesta are arranged for liturgical needs. Only one of the twenty-one divisions of the old book has remained in its original form: the Vendidad, more correctly the Videvdat, or demon-code, which contains mostly prescriptions for preserving or re-establishing ritual purity. A few extracts will illustrate both doctrine and style.

"How long shall land on which dogs and men have died lie fallow?" Ahura Mazda answered, "One year, oh just Zarathushtra, shall land, on which dogs and men had died, lie fallow.

"And worshippers of Mazda should not sow nor water the land on which dogs and men have died for a whole year. If they wish they may sow other land during this time, and, if they wish, they may water it.

"If the worshippers of Mazda, in the course of the year, sow or water the land on which dogs and men have died, the worshippers of Mazda make themselves guilty towards the water, the earth and the plants, of the sin of burying corpses."

"Creator of the material world, just one! If the worshippers of Mazda, during the year, sow or water land on which dogs and men have died, what is their judgement?"

Ahura Mazda answered: "For one who in this way has committed himself shall be prescribed 200 blows of the horsewhip and 200 blows of the scourge."

"Creator of the material world, just one! If the worshippers of Mazda wish to water, plough and return to the land, to cultivate it, how shall the worshippers of Mazda set about it?"

Ahura Mazda answered: "On the land shall the worshippers of Mazda collect up the bones, skins, sticky dejecta, excrement and blood."

"Creator of the world, just one! If the worshippers of Mazda there on the land, do not collect up the bones, skins, sticky dejecta and blood and excrement, what is their punishment?"

Ahura Mazda answered: "For one who in this way has committed himself shall be prescribed 200 blows of the horsewhip and 200 blows of the scourge."

It would certainly seem that these precise, and often lengthy requirements represent, like the "Laws of Manu" in India and other similar codes, an ideal of priestly government rather than the practical reality of any society. Here is another example:

"Creator of the material world, just one! If a worshipper of Mazda wishes to practise the art of healing, upon whom should he try it out at first? upon the worshippers of Mazda or the worshippers of daevas?"

Ahura Mazda answered: "He shall try it out on the worshippers of daevas before doing it on the worshippers of Mazda. If he operates on a worshipper of daevas who dies; if he operates on a second worshipper of daevas who dies, if he operates on a third worshipper of daevas who dies, he will be incapable for always and for ever.

"Let him not, therefore, venture to nurse a worshipper of Mazda, let him not venture to operate on a worshipper of Mazda and wound him during the operation. If he nurses a worshipper of Mazda, if he operates on a worshipper of Mazda and wounds him during the operation, for this wounding he shall pay the penalty for premeditated act.

"If he operates on a worshipper of daevas and heals him; if he operates on a second worshipper of daevas and heals him; if he operates on a third worshipper of daevas and heals him,, he will be capable for always and ever.

"Thereafter, he may, if he wishes, treat the worshippers of Mazda; he may, if he wishes, operate on the worshippers of Mazda and cure them by operating."

It is difficult to imagine the worshippers of daevas giving themselves up as guinea pigs like this. But the intention reveals a splendid arrogance on the part of the worshippers of Mazda.

The rest of the Avesta comprises mainly the Yasna, "Sacrifice", and the Yashts, or hymns. The Yasna is the equivalent of the Roman missal, it is the text which is recited with the sacrifice of fire and *haoma*, the main ceremony of Parsee religion. Three of its seventy-two Chapters, 9, 10 and 11, may be considered as a hymn to Haoma, the god personifying the sacrificial drink. In addition, there are sermons, or *gathas* (etymologically "chants") of the prophet Zarathushtra, inserted in the Yasna rather like the Gospels in the Mass. These are written in a dialect somewhat different from, and more archaic than, the rest of the Avesta. Seventeen in number, they make up Chapters 28–34, 43–51, and 53. They are the principal and almost unique source of our knowledge of the prophet and his doctrine, and nearly the only Iranian work that offers any literary interest. A few extracts will allow the reader to judge for himself.

Yasna 29 is the *gatha* of the Complaint of the ox.

"The soul of the ox complained to you:
For whom have you created me? Who has made me?
Fury, violence, tyranny and cruelty oppress me.
I have no other herd but you; find me then good pastures."

Then the Maker of the ox asked Justice: "Hast thou a patron for the ox, that thou mayest give him, with his pasture, all the cares of divine upbringing?

"What master have you assigned to him to put fury and the wicked to flight?"

Proceeding entreaty by entreaty, the soul of the ox reaches Ahma Mazda who finally tells it:

"I know but one: Zarathushtra Spitama, who alone has heard my teaching; he wishes, wisely, to recite hymns to us and to Justice. He must be given sweetness of speech."

But the soul of the ox is still not satisfied and, through it, all the anxiety of Zarathushtra, still without a protector, emerges:

"Then the soul of the ox groaned: 'Must I then be content with one who cannot realize his plans, with the word of a man without heroism, I, who desire a strong master? Will he ever exist who shall help me with his hands?'"

Yasna 30 may be called the *gatha* of the Choice: it tells of the exemplary choice made at the beginning of the world. Here are four verses (out of eleven), the translation of the first being uncertain:

Now, in the beginning, the two spirits known in dreams as twins,
Are, one good, the other evil,
In thought, word and deed. And between the two,
The intelligent chose well, not the fools.

And when these two spirits met,
In the beginning they established life and non-life,
And that, in the end, the evil should have the worst existence,
But the good, the Better Thought.

Of these two spirits, the evil chose to do the worst things;
But the beneficent spirit, clothed in the strongest skies, rallied to Justice:
And so did all who are glad to support, by honest deeds, the wise Lord.

Between them, the daevas chose not well either,
For error caught them while they yet deliberated,
So that they chose the Worse Thought.

Then they ran to join with Fury, by which men corrupt existence.

Yasna 43 may be called the *gatha* of Conversations with the Lord; here the visions of Zarathushtra are drawn upon, notably the following:

I recognized thy beneficence, O Wise Lord.
When I saw, at the birth of existence, in the beginning,
    that you assigned a recompense for deed and words:
Evil retribution for evil, good for good,
Through thy power, at the last turning of creation.

Yasna 44 may be entitled "Questions to the Lord". Each of its twenty verses, except the last, is begun with this phrase: "This is what I ask thee, Lord—answer me true." Most of these questions are purely rhetorical, as in verses 3–5:

Who at the birth was the first father of Justice?
Who set the sun and stars their roads?
Who is he, if not thou, through whom the moon waxes and
    wanes,
This is what I wish to know, O wise one, and more.

Who set the earth below, and the clouded sky, so that it fall
    not?
Who made fast the waters and plants?
Who harnessed the two chargers to the wind and clouds?
Who, O wise one, is the creator of Good Thought?

What artist made the light and darkness?
What artist sleep and watching?
Who made the morning, noon and even
To show the intelligent man his task?

Yasna 45 seems to be addressed to a larger audience than usual:

I am going to discourse, listen now, and hear,
All of you from near and far, who throng here.

This *gatha* offers, then, a concise summary of the whole doctrine, for the use of the less initiated. Here is one verse, in which the dualist statement matches the monotheism expressed in Yasna 44:

I shall discourse on the two spirits,
Of which the most beneficent, at the beginning of existence,
    said to the destroyer:
"Neither our thoughts, nor doctrines, nor mental powers,
Our choices, words nor deeds,
Neither our essences nor our voices are agreed."

Yasna 56 is the *gatha* of the flight:

To what land shall I flee? Whither to flee, whither to go?
My family and tribe have cast me out;
Neither village nor the evil chiefs of the land support me:
How, O Lord, can I support thee?

I know, O wise one, why I am powerless:
It is because of my lack of flocks and men.
I address my cry to thee: consider it, O Lord,
Granting me the support of one friend for another,
Teach, as well as Justice, the possession of Good Thought.

When, O wise one, will the wills of the saviours to come come
    forth,
Dawns of the days when, by efficient sentences,
The world will uphold Justice,
To whom will help be given, as well as Good Thought?
To me, for I was chosen by thee, O Lord, for revelation.

Finally, two lines from Yasna 50:

"What help may my soul expect from anyone?
I wish to worship you and praise, O Wise Lord.

The *yashts*, or hymns, are equivalent to the "Proper of the Season" in Catholic liturgy. They are hymns recited in honour of this or that divinity, according to the day and the month. They reflect a return to the polytheism from which Zarathushtra had cut free. Of the twenty Yashts (to which the hymn to Haoma, included in the Yasna should be added) the most important are the fifth, to Anahita, the eighth to Tishtrya, the star Sirius, the giver of rain, the tenth to the great god Mithra, the thirteenth to the Fravartis, the nineteenth to the "Royal Glory" (*Khvarnah*), symbol of dynastic authority. A quotation from the hymn to Anahita will suffice to let the reader judge the poetic, narrative and sometimes epic character of these pieces:

The Wise Lord said to Spitama Zarathushtra: O Spitama Zarathushtra, revere for me the wet, heroic and immaculate (goddess) who lies far off, the healer, enemy of the demons, in accord with Ahura, worthy of the reverence of the material world, of the praise of the material world;

She, the just one, who feeds the water courses, the just one who makes the flocks to prosper,

the just one, who makes the living to prosper, the just one who makes the land to prosper,

the just one, who makes the country to prosper,

she who purifies all male seed, who purifies every embryo in the mother's womb up till its birth, who grants easy childbirth, who gives every mother milk at the required moment,

she is the powerful one, heard from afar, who is as great as all the waters stretched out over the earth,

she who flows mightily from Mount Hukairya to Lake Vuru-kasha. . . .

The Paurva, the able sailor, made offering to her, when the conquering hero Thraetona had sent him up into the air in the shape of a vulture.

Three days and nights he flew on and sought to regain his home.

At the end of the third night, he drew near to the shining dawn; at dawn he invoked Ardvi Sura Anahita;

Wet one, heroic and immaculate one, come to my aid!

I shall offer thee a hundred libations of *haoma* and milk, purified and filtered, near the River Rangha, if I return alive to the earth created by Ahura, to my own house.

The wet, heroic and immaculate one hastened towards him, like a lovely young girl, mighty, of splendid stature,

belted high, slender, noble, of high birth,

with shining shoes, with golden laces on her ankles.

She grasped him by the arms and he so did that, quickly

he approached the earth created by Ahura, his own house.

Apart from the Videvdat, the Yasna and the Yashts, the Avesta includes a few other sections of lesser importance.

Whereas the *gathas* are the work of Zarathushtra, the rest of the Avesta ranges through several centuries of development. Further additions were made under the Sassanian king Shapur I. The codification of the various parts under the common name of Apastak, later Avesta, also their writing down, date from the Sassanian period.

The language of the Avesta was no longer a living one after

the fourth century B.C. The sacred text required commentaries
or paraphrases in the common language, i.e. Pahlavi.

PAHLAVI WRITINGS

Pahlavi (or Pehlevi) was the language of the Sassanian
period, the immediate ancestor of modern Persian and the
vehicle of a copious literature, both sacred and profane, produced even under Muslim domination, especially during the
ninth century. The secular literature is almost completely lost
but survives in part in translations or adaptations, in Persian,
like the Book of Kings, the national epic, in Arabic or in other
languages. Religious works included commentaries on the
Avesta and original works. The commentaries were called
Zend, whence the expression *Avesta u Zend*, "Avesta and
Zend", to denote the Book together with its commentaries.
(Western scholars were mistaken when they spoke formerly
of Zend Avesta or of the Zend language.)

The chief original works in Pahlavi are the Denkart, important for its inclusion of a summary, chapter by chapter,
of the lost portions of the Avesta such as it still was at this
time, the ninth century A.D., and the Bundahishn or story of
the beginnings which make use of the lost portions of the
Avesta. An extract is quoted below. Mention must also be
made of the Book of Arda Viraf, a kind of revelation obtained
supposedly by the sage of this name while on a journey
to heaven for the revivification of the faith; the Shkand
Gumanik Vichar or "Decisive Resolution of Doubts" is only
preserved in a transcription into Arabic character (i.e. in
Pazend): it is a book of Mazdaean apologetics, compiled in
the ninth century, which refutes, while supporting dualist ortho-
doxy, the Christian, Manichean, Jewish and Muslim positions.
"The Spirit of Wisdom" (Menok i Khrat) reflects somewhat
the great Zervanist heresy (see below, Zervanism).

The tenor, if not the style, which is very poor, of Pahlavi
writings may be judged from the following beginning of a kind

of catechism: "The Selected Counsels of the Wise Men of Old":

> The wise men of old, in accordance with the revelation of the Religion, said, in their primordial wisdom, that on reaching the age of fifteen every man and woman should know the answers to the following questions: Who am I? To whom do I belong? Whence have I come and whither shall I return? What is my race and lineage? What is my function, what is my duty on earth, and what will be my requital in the world to come? Do I come from the invisible world? What was my position in this world? Do I belong to Omazd or to Ahriman? Do I belong to the gods or the demons? Do I belong to the good or the wicked? Am I man or demon? How many roads are there (to salvation)? What is my religion? Where is my gain, and where my loss? Who is my enemy and who my friend? Is there one first principle or are there two? From whom comes goodness, and from whom evil? Of whom is the light and of whom darkness? From whom comes perfume and from whom stench? From whom is order and from whom disorder? From whom is pardon and from whom the lack of pardon?

AHURA MAZDA

"Wise Lord", the supreme god of ancient Iran, later Ormazd (Ormuzd is an older English transliteration which now gives rise to erroneous pronunciation). He seems to combine the two aspects of the function of sovereignty (see below, Amasha Spantas) and bring about the fusion, conceived by Zarathushtra, of the two gods who before had shared these two aspects. In India there were both Varuna and Mitra. In the Vedi hymn, they form part of the group of gods known as *asuras*, "lords". The *asuras*, as opposed to the gods who were only gods (*devas*, celestial beings), had a more moral, abstract quality. This opposition was marked in India and in Iran but in two different ways. In India, the moral quality became occult, evil, and the *asuras*, in the classical period, became demons, leaving the *devas* as the only gods. In Iran it was the other way round; the *ahuras* monopolized the divine quality to the detriment of the *daevas* who sank to the level of demons.

In this way the pair sometimes called Ahura-Mithra in the Avesta, also the cases in which the second term could have been replaced by Mazda "wise", may correspond exactly to the Indian Varuna-Mitra. The expression Ahura Mazda, still in two words in the *gathas* and in some Achaemenian inscriptions, fused together to form one word in all the others. Ahura-mazda is the great god of the Achaemenians but not their only god. Mithra, especially, occupies an important place, "among the other gods that are".

For Zarathushtra, there is no god but the Wise Lord. He alone possesses power, knowledge and justice, he alone may be invoked as a friend. He is the creator of good and evil, of light and darkness—though he remains, in accordance with his origin, a celestial god. Nevertheless, he does delegate and distribute his powers to some degree to his following of Arch-angels (Amasha Spantas, see below). It is through them that he reigns and governs and leads the struggle against the Evil Spirit, Ahra Mainyu (see below).

After Zarathushtra, polytheism reappears, while Ahura Mazda preserves his position of eminence, at least in ortho-doxy. But he is not the only "worshipped being" in the Avesta, outside the *gathas*; his position is comparable to what he held under the Achaemenians: beside him, Mithra, Anahita, Tish-trya, etc., are all invoked. A new, generic term, *Yazata*, desig-nates conveniently all the "worshipped beings" without obvious offence to monotheistic principles. It might be translated "divinity". In the plural it has abstract value: "the Divinity". This plural, *Yazdan*, later on, when the coming of Islam made it necessary to stress the oneness of God, was the word used to name God or to translate "Allah". The name Ormazd was bound up with the associations not only of polytheistic ideas but, above all, dualistic ones.

AHRIMAN

In ancient times Ahra Mainyu "The Destroyer Spirit", enemy of Spanta Mainyu, "The Beneficent Spirit" (see below, Amasha

Spanta). In Zarathushtra's conception he is the chief of the *daevas*, the prince of darkness, of death, and of lying and deceit, *druj*. All the history of the world is the story of the conflict between Ahriman and Ormazd. Ormazd created the world in order to struggle with this enemy; Ahriman's answer to this good creation was an evil creation. All wicked beings are under his command. At the end of the world, Ormazd will triumph over Ahriman.

The Videvdat preserves the story of the temptation of Zarathushtra by Ahra Mainyu:

From the northernmost end of the earth, the northernmost ends of the earth came Ahra Mainyu, the great destroyer, daeva of all daevas. Thus spoke the cunning Ahra Mainyu, great destroyer: "Druj, go and kill the just Zarathushtra!" The Druj, the daeva Buiti and the peril coming from Marshavan wheeled about him.

Zarathushtra recited the Ahuna-vairiya profession of faith. He venerated the good waters of the good Daitya, and knew that he was of the essence of the worshippers of Mazda. The Druj, beaten, withdrew, and also the daeva Buiti and the peril coming from Marshavan.

The Druj replied: "O Ahra Mainyu, I do not know how to destroy Spitama Zarathushtra, the just Zarathushtra is full of blessing." Zarathushtra sensed his thought: "The cunning daevas, the fellows of the Druj, are gathering to effect my end."

Then Zarathushtra arose, Zarathushtra went forward without yielding to Aka Mana, Bad Thought, to his artfully contrived questions. Now, the just Zarathushtra, holding stones in his hands, as large as houses, which he had received from the creator, Ahura Mazda, stands still. "Where over the wide round earth with far off limits, wilt thou throw these stones that thou holdest at the edge of the Draja, on the hill whereat is the house of Purushapa?"

Zarathushtra replied to Ahra Mainyu: "O artful Ahra Mainyu, I shall strike the creation made by the daevas, I shall strike the Nasu (demon of corpses) made by the daevas, I shall strike Khnanthaiti the sorceress, until the victorious Saoshyant be born from Lake Vurukasha, in the corner east of the world, the corners east of the world."

The artful Ahra Mainyu answered him: "Do not destroy my creation, O just Zarathushtra! Thou art the son of Purushaspa, I was invoked by thy mother. Abjure the good essence of the worshippers of Mazda, so as to gain the same favour as the earthly lord Vadhaghan!"

Spitama Zarathushtra answered him: "I will not abjure the good essence of the worshippers of Mazda, for fear lest my body or vital force be dissolved."

The artful Ahra Mainyu answered him: "With what word wouldst thou conquer, with what word cast off, with what well-made weapon wouldst thou conquer and cast off my creation, coming from the evil spirit?"

Spitama Zarathushtra answered him: "The haoma mortar, and haoma cups and the word that Mazda has proclaimed and the Vahishtam profession of faith are my weapons; with this word will I conquer, with this word will I cast off, with this well-made weapon will I cast off thy creation, artful Ahra Mainyu! Spanta Mainyu created it, created it in endless time; the Amasha Spantas created it, they who reign well and do well . . ."

Mazdaean propaganda was never able to stamp out the cult of Ahriman and the other *daevas*. Mention has been made of the proposition in the Videvdat that worshippers of *daevas* be made the patients of medical students. Xerxes, in an inscription, boasts of replacing the cult of *daevas* by that of Ahuramazda. Plutarch, in his treatises *Isis and Osiris*, tells us that "Zoroaster the Magian taught the Persians to sacrifice offerings of prayers and good deeds to Horomazes, and offerings to Areimantos so as to ward off evil and misfortune. For, crushing a herb called amome in a mortar, they invoke Hades and the darkness: then, having mingled the blood of a butchered wolf, they take it all to a sunless place and leave it". The presence of wolf bones near sanctuaries of the mysteries of Mithra matches perfectly Plutarch's description and testifies to the survival of the cult, further confirmed by dedications *Deo Arimanio*. It is probably Ahriman who is represented as a man with the head of a lion, the body wound round by a snake with two pairs of wings, in statues or reliefs which for a long time have been taken to be the supreme god of the Mysteries. These representations correspond fairly closely to the description of "The Manichean Demon, another form of Ahriman". "His head was that of a lion," says the Arabic book, the *Fihrist*, "his trunk that of a dragon, his wings those of a bird, he had the tail of a great fish, and the feet of a reptile." At the same time, the four wings (the seasons), the snake, the signs of the Zodiac which often adorn the Mithriac leontocephalus prove that it owed something to Zervan (see below, Zervanism) as prince of this world (see below, Gnosticism).

AMASHA SPANTAS

"Beneficent immortals", a term designating in the parts of the Avesta composed after the *gathas*, in which they still have no collective name, those archangels forming, in Zarathushtra's conception, the following of Ahura Mazda. As each one of them is patron of some sphere of the material world, earth, metals, etc., attempts have been made to understand from this their original significance. But the connection is secondary and not found in the *gathas*, their very names indicating their abstract quality. In order to avoid what appeared to contradict a theory of evolution some have tried to trace the personification of sections of society in them. But the final solution has been deduced from comparison of the pantheons of India and ancient Italy.

Since the Indo-Iranian period, social sections had been associated with the various gods who were patrons of the various functions within society. These functions, with their gods and associated sections of society, were organized into an essentially tripartite hierarchy, the origin of which dates back to the Indo-European period. The greatest ramifications of the system are to be found in India.

The most important function, that of sovereignty, had as patrons two principal gods, Varuna, Guardian of Order and Justice, and Mitra "the contract", "the friend". In Zarathushtra's system, Ahura Mazda, the only god, combines the two sides of this function, but the latter persists, like the other functions, in a hierarchy of archangels in which Justice, Asha, holds the highest place, above Vohu Mana, "Good Thought", which holds the position of Mitra. Accessory to the function of sovereignty, Sraosha, "Obedience, Discipline", corresponds in Zarathushtra's system to the Aditya Aryaman of the Veda, and Ashi, "Retribution", to Aditya Bhaga.

The second function, of physical force for fighting, had as patron Indra. With Zarathushtra, Khshathra, "Empire", corresponds to him, while Indra himself persists as a *daeva*, or demon.

The third function, of fecundity, had for patron a variable and multivalent goddess, to whom the archangel Armaiti, "Devotion", corresponds, and by the twin Nasatyas, "Healers", whose counterparts in Iran are the archangels Haurvatat and Amartat, "Health and non-Death", though one of the twins survived there as a demon by the name of Naonhaithya.

Also, there is the god Vayu, "Cosmic wind", a kind of Janus, ruling over ambiguous beginnings, who with Zarathushtra becomes the initial choice between Good and Evil, figured in the two Mainyus or Spirits, Spanta Mainyu, "The Beneficent Spirit", and Ahra Mainyu, "the Destroyer Spirit". For the relations between Vayu and Zervan, god of Time, see below, Zervanism.

Zarathushtra gives a monotheistic and dualistic twist to the system by subordinating all entities to Ahura Mazda and making them the instruments of this god for the fight against the forces of evil. This solidarity is shown by epithets: *spanta*, "beneficent", is not only applied to the god but also to his spirit, Spanta Mainyu, and to devotion, Spanta Armaiti; *vohu*, "good", qualifies Good Thought, Vohu Mana, Good Empire, Vohu Khshathra and, in the superlative, Excellent Justice, Asha Vahishta.

After Zarathushtra, the Archangels tended to be no more than a few odd gods among those re-accepted by Zoroastrianism.

MITHRA

The Iranian form of the name of the Indo-Iranian god known in India as Mitra. Like Mitra with Varuna, Mithra made a pair with an Ahura (see above, Ahura Mazda). He was patron of the human, kindly aspect of sovereignty, as opposed to the terrible, justice-dealing and magical aspect represented by his associate. In different times and places he was at least as popular as Ahura Mazda, except in Zarathushtra's preaching in which he is ignored. The Achaemenians invoked him as well as Ahura Mazda.

In the month of Mithra, the great feast of Mithrakana was celebrated: the king of Persia would always become drunk with a solar crown on his head. The association of Mithra with drunkenness and the sun is most ancient: in a Vedic myth, Mithra refuses to take part, with the other gods, in the ritual murder of the god Soma (see above, Haoma). The reason he gives hints at yet another association: he is afraid of earning the hatred of the oxen (for Soma was identified with the sacrificial ox).

Mithra was probably left out of Zarathushtra's system because of his associations with blood and inebriety. When his cult reappears in the post-*gatha* part of the Avesta, he has lost these compromising characteristics. In the hymn dedicated to him (Yasht 10, see above, Avesta), Mithra is a warrior with white hair (solar association) but he is essentially, as his name implies, the friend and guardian of contract. His function of god of justice again assimilates him to the sun. In eschatology his rôle is that of judge: he is flanked in this by Sraosha, "Discipline" (see above, Amasha Spantas), and Rashnu.

Mithra is qualified by Plutarch as a "mediator". This looks as if it should be taken in several, not necessarily reconcilable ways: "the contract" between the sun and the moon (Yasht 6), intermediary between light and darkness (Al Biruni), or between Ormazd and Ahriman (see below, Zervanism), finally a demiurge, according to a passage in Porphyry.

For the possible rôle played by Mithra in the formation of the Christian idea of a saviour, see below, Iran and Israel.

YIMA

Whereas in the Veda Yama is the first mortal and departer, as the first one to die, he who opens the way to the dead, thereby becoming in India the being of the underworld, to Iran, Yima is the first king and sacrificer and his reign is seen as a golden age. He is called "splendid", *khshaeta*, an epithet that he shares with the sun. As moreover, both in India and Iran he is declared to be the son of Vivasvant-Vivahvant, i.e. the sun, it may be conjectured that in the Indo-Iranian period there was a sun-king who may reasonably be compared with Pharaoh: a primitive concept according to which the king, the doer of all good, prolongs his function and action even in death.

If one may relate Yama with the Germanic Ymir, this hero must have featured in an Indo-European myth in which he was not the sacrificer but the victim. The Edda actually relates that the earth was created from the flesh of Ymir, the sea from his blood, etc. But it was as a sacrificer, "giving the people pieces of beef to eat" (a form of liberality that was a means of government) that Yima was repudiated by Zarathushtra, together with sacrifice itself.

The post-*gatha* part of the Avesta honours in him the sovereign of the golden age and the builder of the shelter in which the living will survive a catastrophic winter, like the one which occurred at the beginning of time. (See Eschatology.) Yima survived in Iranian legend as Jemshid, i.e. "Yima the splendid".

FRAVARTI

In ancient Iranian religion, this term (also Fravashi) was used for the manes, spirits of ancestors or hero–protectors. Ten days at the end of the year were sacred to them, during which they were supposed to come back home to earth. They were offered food and clothing. They were invoked in battle; they presided over generation, pregnancy, childbirth, and by natural extension of the notion of fecundity, over the irrigation of plants:

We venerate the good, powerful and beneficent Fravashis of the just, those who, at the time of Hamaspathmaedya flee here from their dwelling and wander around for ten nights calling out:

"Who will praise us, who will revere us, sing to us, please us, receive us with a hand that offers milk and clothing, and an offering that makes justice be,

by whom will our name be praised, our soul revered,

to whom shall we give the reward for him to keep imperishably for all eternity?"

And the man who reveres them with a hand that offers milk and clothing, and an offering that makes justice be,

him do they bless, the strong Fravashis of the just, for they are satisfied and suffer no hurt nor find hostility.

May there be richness in this house, of men and beasts, may the horse be swift and the chariot solid,

may the man who reveres us with a hand that offers milk and clothing, and an offering that makes justice be,

stand fast in battle and defy the enemy!

We revere the good, powerful and beneficent Fravashis of the just, who are greater, stronger, braver, more victorious, more healing and more helpful in the final trial than words can express, who fly in thousands towards offerers of gifts and surround them.

And when the waters rise up from Lake Vurukasha, O Spitama Zarathushtra, like the Glory created by Mazda, then do the strong Fravashis of the just draw near in thousands, in tens of thousands,

to look for water, each for her family, her village, canton and country, saying: Our country may perish and dry up.

They struggle in battle for their homeland and country, where each has her home and hearth, as a brave warrior would defend with weapons the land he has justly inherited.

This concept, implying no idea of moral excellence, or of division between the good and wicked, was for that very reason ignored by Zarathushtra. The explanation is wrong therefore which would make the Fravashis signify, etymologically, the Zoroastrian choice between good and evil—and thereby explain the name Fravartish, in Greek Phraortes, as "Confessor" (of Zoroastian religion).

It appears to have been proved, not long ago, that the Fravashis belonged to the second function: warrior and sorcerer spirits, they may recall the Indian Maruts, or the Valkyries in Germanic mythology.

Zoroastrianism could not adopt the Fravashi idea without modifying it. Only the Fravashis of the just were taken into account. Besides, the disciples of Zarathushtra, being unable to admit that their prophet had not pre-existed before his arrival on earth, spoke of his Fravashi of former days. This idea was made general and a Fravashi was given to every man before his birth. The generalization was pushed even further and the term came to mean a kind of celestial double not only of corporal creatures but of deities also: Ahura Mazda himself had his Fravashi.

The idea of a choice, partly due to the false etymology referred to above, was associated with the Fravashis: in the Bundahishn, a Pahlavi treatise on the Beginnings, the Fravashis, before their terrestrial birth, are presented with the choice between incarnation into the world, there to struggle against Deceit, and staying sheltered in the celestial world. They choose to be born and to struggle:

He (Ormazd) united thought to the consciences and Fravashis of men and produced in them clear-sighted minds, saying, "What seems more profitable to you, that I should create you in the visible world and that you should fight in corporal form against Deceit, and destroy Deceit, that in the end I should establish you hale and immortal and restore you to the visible world and that you should be immortal for ever, free from old age and enemies; or that I grant you eternal protection against the enemy?" The Fravashis of men saw in their clear-sighted minds that Deceit and Ahriman would bring them distress in the visible world but also, finally, liberation from the snares of their enemy, and because of this re-establishing in integrity and immortality for always in the future body, they agreed to come down into the visible world.

ESCHATOLOGY

Before Zarathushtra, the Iranians, like many ancient peoples, believed in a return of the golden age. First of all a catastrophic winter would come upon the earth. The human race would only survive, like the animal and vegetable species as of old, by means of a refuge built by Yima, by which the new earth would be repopulated. Zarathushtra announces the definite coming of a new world and the triumph of the forces of good over the forces of evil.

Beliefs in the survival of the individual developed parallel to this general eschatology. In the oldest Indo-Iranian conception, which may be gathered from the Veda, the home of the dead, the kingdom of a Yama appears sometimes as a paradise of light, sometimes as a sinister, underground, infernal abyss, entered by a way sloping downwards. Happiness after death appears to be a privilege of the great, of heroes. It seems that according to the primitive conception of the Iranians, found in various primitive peoples, the blessed state in the next world is reserved for those who are clever and skilful enough to cross a bridge.

Zarathushtra, while adopting the old bridge myth, remoulds it to his demand for justice and calls it the Bridge of the Requiter (Bridge of the Chinvant); he also has an individual judgement of souls at the entrance to the bridge—which is now no more than an accessory part of the scenery.

In the post-*gatha* Avesta, general eschatology and other beliefs concerning life after death are brought into harmony by means of two innovations: one is the development of a chronology which places the transfiguration of the world at a very much later date than the first pronounced, the immediate future; the other belief is the resurrection. According to the new plan, the soul is judged straight after death, crosses, or fails to cross, the Bridge of Retribution and goes to Heaven or to Hell (or, if its good actions equal its bad ones, to an intermediate place), till the day when the bodies rise again for a general ordeal by fire and for the definitive reign of God in a renewed world.

The fate of the soul is the subject of a moving story:

At the end of the third night, when dawn appeared, the soul of the just man thinks that it is among plants and breathing perfumes. It seems as if there blows towards it, from southern lands, a fragrant wind, more fragrant than any other.

And the soul of the just man seems to breathe this wind into its nose and to say: "Whence does this wind blow, more sweet-smelling than all those that my nostrils have ever breathed?"

At the coming of this wind, the soul's own essence appears to it in the form of a beautiful young girl, with white arms, strong, fine of face, slender, with full, firm breasts, noble form, high birth and glorious lineage, seemingly fifteen years old and of more lovely shape than the loveliest of creatures.

And the soul of the just man asks her: "What maid art thou, O fairest of all maids that I have ever seen?"

And his own essence answers: "O thou, young man of good thought, good word, good deed and good essence, I am thy own essence".

"And who has loved thee for this majesty, this goodness, this beauty, this perfume, this victorious strength, this power over enemies, with which I see thee appear to me?"

"O young man of good thought, good word, good deed and good essence, it is thou who hast loved me for the majesty, goodness, beauty, perfume, victorious strength and power over enemies with which thou seest me appear.

"When thou sawest anyone burn the dead and worship idols, oppress others and cut down trees, then didst thou sit down to sing the *gathas*, sacrifice to the good waters and the fire of Ahura Mazda and welcome the just men coming from near or far.

"Therefore, being lovable, thou hast made me more lovable; beautiful, thou hast made me more beautiful, desirable, thou hast made me still more desirable; seated in a high place, thou hast set me in a place still higher."

As for the last judgement, the date of this is settled in advance, for it is only the last phase of a vast, cosmic drama, regularly divided into equal periods, each one three thousand years long. In the first period, the world has not yet come into existence. Everything is only under heavenly conditions; the period of the Fravashis.

After the first period of 3000 years, beings are created in their corporeal forms. These are, notably, the primeval man, known as Mortal Life (Gayomart), and the ox, "the first creature". In answer to this creation, Ahriman produces, in turn, his own counter creation. Notable parts of this creation are the planets, whereas the stars are creatures of Ormazd.

The third millennium is marked by Ahriman's bursting into the creation of Ormazd after being kept powerless by a magic formula. He kills Gayomart from whom humanity and the metals appear, and the ox, who gives birth to animals and plants.

The beginning of the last period witnesses the coming of religion on earth, namely the birth of Zarathushtra. The end of each millennium will be marked by the coming of a new Saviour, successor and miraculous descendant of Zarathushtra. (See below, Saoshyant.) The last of them will bring about the last judgement and the arrival of a new world.

SAOSHYANT

"Future Saviour", the term by which Zarathushtra referred to those who, by their virtue and struggle against the forces of evil, help him to bring about the kingdom of Ahura Mazda.

In the Yashts of the Avesta, the term has a certain eschatological sense. The Saoshyant, named Astvat-arta, "Order, or Justice Incarnate", is destined to bring about the end of the world, will be born of a virgin from the seed of Zarathushtra, miraculously preserved in a lake, guarded by 99,999 Fravashis. Two companions of this Saoshyant, Ukhshyat-arta, "Enlarging justice" and Ukhshyat-nama, "Enlarging reverence", are mentioned by name in Yasht 13. According to later tradition they will appear 1000 and 2000 years respectively after Zarathushtra; they too will be of the race of Zarathushtra.

The account of this future salvation is shot through with another idea, for which we may use a term taken from St Irenaeus—recapitulation. The happenings of the beginning of the world will be reproduced in reverse order and with opposite values. Thus, the first human pair fed first on water, then on plants, then on milk, and finally, by the grace of Yima, on meat. So, the men of the last millennia, at the coming of each Saoshyant will renounce, in reverse order, meat, milk, plants, keeping to water only in the end. Cosmogonic murders, especially of the ox, will be renewed in eschatology. The ox Hadhayosh will be sacrificed for his fat or marrow, and from white Hom (Haoma) the drink of immortality will be made. The dragon Azhi Dahaka will be killed by Feridun (Thraetona), as it was in the beginning. Finally, Gayomart (see above, Eschatology) will re-appear also in an eschatological rôle: as he was the first man, so will he be the first to rise again.

ZERVANISM

An Iranian doctrine which has Zervan, "the Time", as its supreme god. It is not certain whether or not this god is attested in the twelfth century B.C. text of the Nuzi cuneiform tablets. Eight centuries later, the Babylonian Berosus speaks of a "mythical king Zerovanus", while Eudemus of Rhodes, a pupil of Aristotle, tells of a philosopher. His account—related by the neo-Platonist Damascius—seems to be the answer to a question put by a Greek impressed by Iranian dualism: "What is the supreme and sole principle?" But the reply is ambiguous, for, beside Time, Space is also quoted as a name of the "infinite and intelligible all".

What can the relationship have been of this god of Time with primeval Space, and especially with the Cosmic Wind, Vayu, the Iranian Janus, double god of ambiguous beginnings?

Recent research, which has discovered Zervan and Vayu in epic, disguised as heroes (Zal and Rustam), gives the idea that the former was father to the latter.

Zarathushtra cannot have ignored the god of Time and Destiny, who had made sacrifice to get offspring, nor Vayu, his son, patron of beginnings and master of life and death. He had no need of the former, once he had conceived his own god, Ahura Mazda, as a synthesis of the justice and goodness of the ruler. He had no room for a god of fate in a system that rejects fatalism utterly. But something of Vayu was able to remain: his two opposed halves, under another form, were derived from old myths about the primeval twins, to illustrate the great idea of the Choice.

The appearance of astral fatalism in Iran, some centuries after Zarathushtra, seems to be due to Greco-Babylonian influence which gave new vigour to the old faith in the Time God.

At all events, this fatalism seems to have been the religion of the people under the Arsacids and Sassanids, against which official Mazdaism had to sustain a long struggle in the Sassanian period, with varying success. The supreme god of Manicheism is Zervan, not Ormazd: the supremacy of Ormazd was more theoretical than real.

Official doctrine, reflected in the Avesta, tries to place Time, Space and Vayu under the supreme authority of Ahura Mazda. In the Videvdat, Zervan is more a principle than a god. He is described as imperishable and infinite. When he appears in more concrete form, it is as god of the three ages of man and as god of death. More recently composed passages of the Avesta distinguish, with more sagacity, between Time "without limit" (*a-karana*), and Time "long to rule".

Zervanism and Mazdaism could be combined in two ways. As we have seen above, Zervan may be absorbed into the dualist system of official Mazdaism; or else Zervan may keep the highest position and take on certain Mazdaean features. This is illustrated by the myth of Zervan, giving birth to the twins

Ormazd and Ahriman, recorded by the Armenian Esnik, writing in the fifth century A.D.:

When as yet nothing was, say the Iranians, neither heavens nor earth, nor any other creatures whatever that are found in the heavens and on the earth, there was one called Zruan, which is interpreted as "Fate" or "Glory".

For a thousand years he had been making sacrifice so that he might have a son, whose name would be Ormizd and who would make the heavens and the earth and all that is contained therein. For a thousand years he had made sacrifice, when he began to ponder and said: "What use can the sacrifice that I make have? Shall I have a son Ormizd? Or are all my efforts in vain?"

And while he pondered thus, Ormizd and Ahrmn were conceived in the womb of their mother, Ormizd by virtue of the sacrifice and Ahrmn by virtue of the doubt: Then, realizing what had happened, Zruan said:

"Two sons are in that womb; the one who comes sooner to me, whichever he be, him shall I make king."

When Ormizd learnt of their father's plan, he revealed it to Ahrmn, saying: "Zruan our father has made this plan: whichever of us comes sooner to him, he will make king."

And when Ahrmn heard this he pierced the womb and came out, and showed himself to his father. And Zruan seeing him did not know who he could be; so he asked, "Thou, who art thou?"

And he said, "I am thy son."

Zruan said to him: "My son is sweet smelling and lightsome and thou art darksome and stinkest."

And while they exchanged these words, Ormizd was born in due time, lightsome and sweet smelling, and came to show himself to Zruan. And when Zruan saw him, he knew that it was his son Ormizd, for whom he had made sacrifice. Taking the rods which he had in his hand, with which he made sacrifice, he gave them to Ormizd and said: "Till now, it was I who offered sacrifice for thee, henceforth thou shalt offer it for me."

And while Zruan was giving the rods to Ormizd and blessing him, Ahrmn drew near to Zruan and said to him: "Hast thou not vowed this vow: whichever of my sons comes sooner to me, him shall I make king?"

And Zruan, that he might not break his word, told Ahrmn: "O knave and evil doer! Royal state will be granted to thee for nine thousand years and [=but] Ormizd, I have made king above thee and, after nine thousand years, Ormizd will reign, and all that he would do, he will do."

Then Ormizd and Ahrmn began to make creatures. And all that Ormizd created was good and straight, and all that Ahrmn made was bad and twisted.

PARSEEISM

The religion of the Parsees, Iranian emigrants in India where, in Gujerat and Bombay, they form a very prosperous community of about 100,000 persons. They are most ready to accept modern civilization and are distinguished for their enterprising spirit, in finance, business and industry, and for the number of their schools, hospitals and other good works.

Their most striking rite is the exposure of the dead in "Towers of Silence". The native name for these structures, meaning etymologically "stake", proves that, before adopting this tradition, attested in antiquity among the Magians, the Iranians practised incineration. Moreover, it is known that the kings of Persia, at the time of Cyrus, Darius, etc., neither burnt nor left their dead exposed to the birds, but embalmed them and buried them. Another custom, consanguineous marriage, has fallen into disuse and has been formally disavowed.

The main ceremony of the cult, apart from funerary rites, is the fire and *haoma* sacrifice, practised in the fire temples. The priest, armed with the ritual rods, covers his mouth with a veil intended to protect the sacred fire and liquids from any impurity. This gives him the curiously modern look of "men in white". The ceremony includes the recitation of a large portion of the Avesta.

The Parsees are dualist but, under the influence of Islam, Christianity and Hindu mysticism, they insist on the supremacy of Ormazd. An allegorical interpretation reduces Ahriman to hardly more than a symbol, representing the evil tendencies to be found in man. Their moral code is definitely anti-ascetic:

they preach fecundity, work and cleanliness. They make much of mercy, but, in principle, this does not extend beyond the circle of believers.

In principle also, the believer will be rewarded in the next world strictly in proportion to his good deeds. He can at any time repent of his sins by reciting a confession formula called *patet*, and prayers for the salvation of the dead play a large part in Parsee piety, as they do, sometimes, in their liturgical controversies.

CHAPTER XIII

EXTERNAL RELATIONSHIPS

IRAN AND GREECE

Whereas the Jews, the chosen people, never acknowledged any foreign influence in their religion, the Greeks aspired quite early to the title of heirs of the ancient wisdom of the east. But the more remote in time are the references of their authors to these pretended borrowings the more accurate they are. Indeed there are striking likenesses of doctrine between Iran and Greece. Leaving aside for the present the Hellenistic period and the appearance of Gnosticism, it is still possible to list the following: dualism, the deification of time, the division of world history into definite periods, the notion of a world soul, fire as a symbol of cosmic law, and the pre-existence of ideal models of things. What is the explanation of these resemblances?

Heraclitus, who seems to have insisted on the place of struggle in the world, whom Hegel and Marx take to be their precursor, nevertheless believed in a Logos or Nomos. The essence of this intelligible law was fire. This cannot fail to remind us of the Indo-Iranian connection of fire with justice or order in the world. Other features in Heraclitus' thought have been considered to display an Iranian tendency: his scorning of anthropomorphic images and bloody sacrifice, and his dislike of corpses which he deems should be thrown into the offal heap. The comparison is clearly an exaggeration, for what has the Magian rite of exposing bodies in common with Heraclitus' hostility towards any funeral rite whatever? Heraclitus opposes all religious practices. On two points does he agree with the

Iranian attitude: the lack of divine images and the condemnation of bloody sacrifice. But this latter feature is common to many people at a certain stage of development, and another feature of Heraclitus is quite opposed to Zarathushtra's doctrine: he makes no exception in the case of fire worship which Zarathushtra glorifies. Their agreement on fire as the symbol of universal order may nevertheless be accidental. One thinker or the other may have taken over a common inheritance—the notion of world order, already explicitly stated in Greece and expressed in Indo-Iranian by the term *Rta-Asha*, with which the vision of omnipresent fire was associated.

With Plato, the distinction between mind and matter was typically Greek, being derived from a multiple tradition— Ionian, Pythagorean, Eleatic and Sophistic. The opposition of mind and matter had already been transferred to the epistemological sphere, between physical science and mathematical science. Here, Plato's position differed essentially from Zarathushtra's. For the Iranian prophet, the distinction was only between visible things and the superior realities to which his ecstasies, meditation and devotion provided access. He certainly had no idea of the critical problem.

The Platonic doctrine of the soul, set out in mythical form in the *Timaeus*, was taken in a monist, optimistic sense: evil is the absence of God and the individual is free to choose. Plato would never hear of two spirits, one good and the other evil. He expressly rejects this idea in the course of his myth in *The Politics*: the world goes between good and evil like a wheel turning forwards and backwards. Now this cannot be due to the action of two different gods, but only to the fact that the world obeys, now divine impulse, now itself. Plato may allude to Iranian doctrine, but only to refute it. In the *Laws* in fact he seems to believe for a moment in the possibility of an evil soul, but this is more a plurality of souls than the soul of the world, for this can be nothing but good.

Plato frequently tends to be judged through Gnosticism. It is true that he had the stuff of a pessimistic, anticosmic dualist in him: the *Phaedo,* for instance, is tinged with *Weltflucht*,[1]

---

[1] Escapism.

But one cannot proceed from there to consider that Plato poses the Soul of the world purposely as a bridge over the gulf between God and the world; Plato never felt so great a distance between God and the world as to warrant a third term to link them; for him, the Soul of the World, a traditional idea, was to be deduced from contemplation of the world order, as was God; it was, once more like God, the reason, the *nous*, the harmony of the spheres without which the world order would remain inexplicable.

However, a dualism more ancient than Plato himself does subsist in Plotinus and all the Neo-Platonists: matter or evil is a separate principle, irreducible to God. The Neo-Platonists could therefore legitimately find the roots and seeds of their own attitudes in the *Weltflucht* and profound dualism of the master. The problem is to know what importance to assign this feature in an appreciation of the whole of Plato's doctrine.

A parallel problem occurs with Zarathushtra: is it possible to trace the origin of the Gnostic movement back to him and to the *gathas*? But since the question of the origins of Gnosticism concern not only Iran and Greece, but Palestine also, before it is dealt with the relations between Iranian religion and Judaism must be discussed.

IRAN AND ISRAEL

The debt of Israel to its neighbours in religious matters is easy to demonstrate on a few precise points of minor importance; it is less so in other, more important, points like dualism, angelology and eschatology.

Yahweh was raised so high and so purified by the prophets that the need was felt to bridge the void between his transcendence and the world. The Logos, borrowed from Greek philosophy, was the solution that occurred to Philo. Otherwise, the Wisdom of God is mentioned in Proverbs, Ecclesiasticus, the Book of Wisdom, Enoch, etc. It is the beloved and counsellor of the Lord, the friend and guide of men. Its intrusion into Judaism is so abrupt that one is prompted to imagine a foreign influence. But it is most difficult to find its prototype in Iranian religion. Is it Vohu Mana, "Good Thought", or Armaiti, "Devotion"?

The Spirit is comparable to Spantu Mainyu, and so are the six powers of God in Philonian speculation to the Iranian archangels. Since the latter were known to the Greeks, it is by no means impossible that Philo had heard about them. In fact, he mentions as quite familiar the Persian doctrine of God's virtues. But the likeness is limited to general analogy. The case of post-exilic soteriology is quite different.

After the Exile, the traditional hope in a Messiah-king of the house of David, who would re-establish Israel as an independent nation and make it triumph over all enemies, gave way gradually to a concept at once more universal and more moral. The salvation of Israel was still essential; but it had to come about in the framework of a general renewal: the appearance of a Saviour would mean the end of this world and the birth of a new creation: his judgement of Israel would become a general judgement, dividing mankind into good and evil.

This new concept, at once universal and ethical, recalls Iran so strongly that many scholars attribute it to the influence of that country, all the more because there is no strong personality to be found in Israel during the last few centuries before our era who could have provoked so profound a change.

However, the resemblance between the Messiah and the Saoshyant is still vague and general, unless the following points are included in the comparison: the notion of an eschatological saviour seems bound up with that of a primeval man, in Iran as well as in certain streams of Judaism. Besides which, the saviour is himself the victim whereby mankind is redeemed.

Firstly, may the Son of Man be compared to Gayomart? The former, as he appears in Daniel, Enoch, etc., seems a purely eschatological figure, quite distinct from the primeval being alluded to by Job and Ezechiel (Job 15. 7–8; "Art thou the first man that was born, or wast thou made before the hills? Hast thou heard God's counsel?" Ezechiel 28, 2 sq: "Because thy heart is lifted up and thou hast said: I am God, and I sit in the chair of God", etc.). On the Iranian side, Gayomart, an essentially cosmogonic figure, is only attested in an eschatological rôle in the Pahlavi books. The fact that the Avesta places him in the same series as Zarathushtra and the Saoshyant by no means implies that all three were considered to be a single being, or even to belong to the same line of descent.

As for the second point, the saviour notion, whatever the time of appearance in Judaism or its affinity with the very widespread idea of the Just Sufferer, its only appearance in Iran, except for a late and dubious reference, is in the Manichean system. The origin of Manicheism is a complicated one, to which Iran makes but a limited contribution.

A third possible point of comparison lies in Mithraism. However, the principal relevant document, a passage in the *Opus Imperfectum in Matthaeum* of Pseudo-Chrysostom, is suspected, like all the commentaries and paraphrases of this sort, of being a forgery made to support the Gospel narrative; even if it is authentic, it only goes back to the fourth century A.D.; moreover the allusion to Mithra is very veiled: at first the picture seems to be made from first-hand knowledge: "The Magians climbed a certain mountain there, called in their language Victory Mountain, in which there was a stone grotto, adorned with fountains and select trees; after reaching this and washing themselves, they prayed and praised God for three days; and so had it been done, generation unto generation, all hoping that their own would see the rising of their famous star of blessedness. . . ." But in what follows something spoils the Mithraistic atmosphere of the scene: "it appeared to them coming down onto Victory Mountain, having within it the image, as it were, of a little child, and above, that of a cross."

Even the *Oracle of Hystaspes*, certainly earlier than the second century of our era, still seems too late, even in its supposed Iranian original, to be adduced as a source of Jewish or Christian apocalyptic literature. Finally, it must not be forgotten, when we compare Mithraism with early Christianity, that our oldest monuments of the mysteries of Mithra date, at the earliest, to the second century A.D.

Did Iranian dualism colour Israel's beliefs at all? A considerable change came about in the conception of Satan. Whereas in the prologue of Job and the mouth of Zacharias, he was no more than the humble servant of God, whose function was to act as prosecutor, he afterwards became God's adversary. Two successive versions of the same story, in Samuel and then in Paralipomenon, show Satan literally taking the place of God. Samuel (2 Kings 24. 1) tells us that the anger of the Lord was kindled against Israel and he stirred David to number his people. Instead of which, in Paralipomenon we read, "And Satan rose up against Israel and moved David to number Israel".

In apocalyptic literature, too, it is possible to follow the progress of the newcomer. The Jewish apocalypses—which are not part of the Old Testament—spoke at first of a judgement of rebellious angels, of the sons and spirits of Belial and Mastema, as well as of those angels who had misused their power of punishment; later, in the assumption of Moses, the final decision is conceived as a struggle between God and the Demon; then, in Sybilline literature and the assumption of Isaias, Belial appears as God's adversary.

All this implies a pessimistic view which may be due partly to the misfortunes of Israel under Greek and Roman domination, but it would be rash to deny that the example of the Iranian Demon helped the Jews to transform the old public prosecutor into the adversary of God. A still more exact parallel is provided by the doctrine of the Two Spirits.

Before the discovery of the Dead Sea Scrolls in 1947, we possessed only scanty traces of this doctrine in Jewish literature. We know that the spirit of Yahweh was not always good and kindly. In Judges we read of an evil spirit that God sends between Abimelech and the inhabitants of Sichem. When the spirit of Yahweh abandons Saul an "Evil Spirit of Yahweh"[2] seizes him.

In apocryphal literature, both primitive Christian and Rabbinical, the good and evil spirits oppose one another: the

[2] I.e. an evil spirit permitted to intervene by Yahweh

Testament of Judas speaks of two spirits that serve men, one of truth and one of error; then it mentions a third spirit which personifies the power of choice: "And in the middle is the spirit of intelligence, to whom it belongs to turn where it wishes". In general only the good and evil spirits are mentioned; in Hermas they are called the holy spirit and the evil spirit which live together in man.

Besides these laconic mentions, the *Manual of Discipline* found in the Dead Sea Scrolls provides us with a whole, small treatise on the two spirits. First of all the fact is stressed that God made everything. Then:

> He created man to rule over the earth and made two spirits for him, with whom he might walk until the day of his coming; they are the spirits of truth and error. The origins of truth are in the abode of light and the origins of error are in the source of darkness. The power over the sons of the light is in the hands of the prince of lights; in the way of light do they walk. And all power over the sons of error is in the hands of the angel of darkness; and in the way of darkness do they walk. And because of the angel of darkness all the sons of justice go astray, and all their sins, all their iniquities, all their rebellions and their works are the result of his power.

> But God, in the mysteries of his intelligence and glorious wisdom, has ordained a time for the downfall of error and, at the moment fixed for the punishment, he will destroy it for ever. Then the truth of the world will appear for evermore....

One's first thought is of the doctrine of the two spirits in the *gathas*, the ethical and eschatological dualism of which can be detected here. But the predestination of the two spirits in the Jewish document is contrary to Zoroastrian free choice.

True, the divergence here could be due to an adaptation of the Iranian myth into the context of Jewish religion; the fact that Yahweh is proclaimed creator of the two spirits, contrary to the doctrine of the Avesta, both of the *gathas* and later, may be explained in the same way. Nevertheless, the survival of a pure *gatha*-type doctrine right up to the time of the *Manual* would present something of a problem in itself, given the

changes that came about in Iranian religion after the time of
its prophet.

Indeed, one feature at least has a source other than the
gathas: the identification of the good spirit with light and of
the bad with darkness, for which the *gathas* provide but a
modest, if imposing, starting point: "He who first thought
how the fortunate spaces are filled with lights" (Yasna 31. 7).

This encourages us to look for another Iranian source, outside the *gathas*, in order to explain the absence in the Jewish
document of what was the very essence of the message of the
gathas: the part of the two spirits as actors in the drama of
the Choice. (Note that this function is so foreign to them in
the Testament of Judas, quoted above, that it was found
necessary to attribute it to a third spirit.)

Finally, by way of summary, predestination in contrast to
free choice, the identification of the two spirits with light and
darkness and, in addition the explicit creation of these spirits
by God, brings us back to the Zervanist myth of a god of time
or fate, father of light Ormazd and the dark Ahriman. Since
this is the form under which, *a priori*, the Jews must have
known Iranian religion at the time, our conjecture is confirmed.

This is corroborated besides by what we know, from Flavius
Josephus, of the part played by Destiny in the religion of the
Essenes, and, thanks to the Dead Sea Scrolls, of the importance
of fates and fixed times among the sectarians of the New
Covenant. To quote Josephus: "The sect of the Essenes holds
that Destiny is master of everything, that nothing happens to
man except what is decreed by him" (*Jewish Antiquities*, 13, 5.9).
The relevant passages from the *Manual of Discipline* and Psalms
of thanksgiving: "Thou hast cast an eternal fate for man" ...
"And according to the heritage of each man in truth he does
good and hates error; but according to his possession of a
share of error he acts evilly and abhors truth" ... "Under their
direction will each fate be ruled for each case having reference
to the law, riches, justice, etc." The synagogue of Bet Alpha
is brought to mind, the mosaic of which features a zodiac.

In contrast with the massive monotheism of the prophets

the concept of Satan as being the antagonist of God and the doctrine of the two spirits represented a step towards pessimism; a new stage was marked when Satan was called "The king of this age", or "the prince of this world". A similar stage is found in Zervanism when Zervan, at the end of the myth, tells Ahriman, "I have made Ormazd king above thee", meaning that Ahriman is prince of this world, but Ormazd reigns in the heavenly world of the spirit. It is also possible to suppose the existence of the same concept in Mithraism, if, as mentioned above (Ahriman), the lion-headed deity is none other than Ahriman, represented, with his snake, his signs of the zodiac and four wings, as master of this world. This concept is also found in Gnosticism.

Of all the other points of comparison between Iran and Israel, namely the doctrine of millennia, the last judgement, the heavenly book in which human actions are inscribed, the resurrection, the final transformation of the earth, paradise on earth or in heaven, the ecstatic ascent of Enoch and Arda Viraf into the heavens, hell, the souls of the animals accusing man in the Slavonic Enoch, like the soul of the ox in the *gathas* and, finally, in Tobias, the demon Asmodeus, alias *aeshma daeva*, the last are the most characteristic.

Several Jewish texts place paradise in the heavens, and are often categoric—the third heaven. Can we assert with any certainty that this goes back to the three places of "Good thoughts, good words and good deeds" of Zoroastrian doctrine? The latter, however, includes a fourth, beyond the three others: the abode of Ahura Mazda or of infinite light (the first three corresponding, respectively, in ascending order, to the stars, the moon and the sun). Why did the Jews adopt only three? The number four is only found in the Talmud, and besides, the number of heavens is sometimes five or seven. There is therefore no question of borrowing from Mazdaean doctrine.

However, the principle of the superposition of the heavens is noteworthy. This may well be a reflection of Shamanic practices, ecstatic ascensions, such as are known to many peoples. A similar journey, to three successive heavens, is

actually attested in Jewish literature, in Chapters 70 to 71 of
the book of Enoch. The prophet goes first to visit the souls of
the dead; then he goes among the angels, becoming an angel
himself; and finally to "the heaven of heavens" where God is.
There is no analogous description on the side of Iran, except
in the Pahlavi work, the Book of Arda Viraf. But it seems that
in ancient times Shamanism was not unknown, at least to some
Iranians. According to Herodotus (4. 75) the Scythians used to
become intoxicated with the fumes of hemp and shouted with
joy and delirium. It has been said that Zarathushtra himself
was a kind of Shaman. In short, as the nearest country to
Palestine in which Shamanism is attested is Iran, it is possible,
but no more, that an Iranian doctrine, not necessarily Avestic,
is at the bottom of the tale of Enoch, and indeed of the more
general belief in several heavens.

Hell, the future home of the resurrected wicked as well as
the souls of the wicked after death, first appears in Jewish
tradition as *ge hinnom*, the galley of refuse (our own *gehenna*).
It seems too much to see in this some recollection of the valley
crossed by the "Bridge of the Recompenser"; also, the darkness of the Jewish hell (Enoch, etc.) is in no way specifically
Iranian. As for the fire (Enoch, IV Esdras, etc.). nothing comparable is to be found in Iran except the fire of the final
ordeal and purification. It should be observed that this element,
so essential to the Jewish hell, only appears rather late as a
characteristic of the Iranian hell, together with others, such
as cold (Datistan i Denik 33. 2–4). The fact that there are angels
present in both cases is no more of a proof, for they only
appear in Iran with the book of Arda Viraf.

The evolution of post-exilic Judaism never resulted in a
completely coherent system. Thus, according to Enoch (45.
4–5), the end of the world will see "a new heaven and a new
earth", but this earth will remain the home of the risen just,
while, in other texts (II Baruch, etc.), they will exist in heaven,
"in the splendour of the angels". But this discrepancy is not
in itself a proof of foreign influence. It is due to elements from
different levels of civilization becoming combined.

Many of these elements, among others depending on universalist, individualist, or philosophical leanings, are the various manifestations of dualism: for instance, the last judgement, a Paradise and Hell, the transformation of the world, not forgetting the advancement of the Adversary, nor his final defeat.

On some points, direct Iranian influence, and not just general analogy, does seem probable.

Here, for example, is a passage from the Slavonic Enoch, chapter 58:

> In the days of our father Adam, the Lord God came down on to the earth and visited his creatures, which he had created himself, and the Lord God called all the beasts of the earth and all the wild animals. . . . In this (world) there will be no judgement of any living soul, save of man only. But for the souls of the beasts there will be a place and a home in the great aeon. For no soul of animal created by the Lord shall be shut up till the great judgement, and all souls shall accuse man. Whoever sullies the soul of a beast, whoever feeds ill the soul of a beast, sullies his own.

Otto saw clearly that "the complaint-accusation of the animal soul, specially the cow, against all injustice inflicted on it by man, is in the *gathas*. Created before all time," he adds, "the soul of the pure animal is before God."

Final mention must be made of the devil Asmodeus, in the book of Tobias (part of the action of which takes place in Iran). It is difficult to explain him other than as a reflection of the Fury daeva, Aeshma (daeva), known to Zarathushtra. (The phonetic correspondence is not exact but this is common in the case of borrowing.)

IRANIAN ORIGINS AND GNOSTICISM

As the definition of Gnosticism as an acute Hellenization of Christianity is now recognized as insufficient, the problem of Iranian origins has been tackled, firstly, by comparing the notion of salvation in Iran and India. It appears to be essentially the same in both, coming from man's desire to transcend the world and unite his soul with the Great Soul.

But, on the Iranian side, the proofs for this pessimistic and anti-cosmic tendency, which are not usually attributed to Iran, are indeed scanty, and it must be admitted that it was largely overlaid or arrested by Zarathushtra's optimistic and ethical dualism.

The means of salvation were present in the *gatha* system itself, in the form of man's union with the Archangels, especially that of his Vohu Mana (*Manwahmed*).

The rôle of Vohu Mana is attested in later Mazdaism, in the Videvdat, in which Vohu Mana receives the soul into heaven and goes with it to the throne of Ahura Mazda.

There remains one last clue in the inquiry, perhaps the strongest of all: the Syriac allegory of the Pearl, which has been summarized as follows: "The pearl which he saves indicates the collective soul redeemed from matter, the sum of all souls to be saved. The redeemer therefore goes down into matter to save the soul, but, if he is to fulfil his work of redemption, he must himself be redeemed from the power of material existence."

It has lately been recognized that this Syriac tale goes back to an Iranian original of the Parthian period. But this does not exclude the possibility of an accidental or Babylonian origin. The Gnostic myth owed something to the story of Tammuz, who comes down, fights, suffers and is imprisoned before rising again.

However it may be, traces are found in Iran of an attitude surviving from the Indo-Iranian past, obscured by the active and ethical dualism of Zarathushtra, but capable of revival. To conclude, Iran was like Greece in possessing, besides a more optimistic conception, an anti-cosmic tendency which could give rise to Gnosticism. However, on each side, this tendency had distinctive features: in Greece, first of all, the identification of the spirit with good and of matter with evil, and secondly, the view of the world as a scale of degrees going from pure aether to pure matter, a ready-made framework for the idea or myth of the fall, fall of the angels, fall of the soul, descent of the saviour and the corresponding re-ascent into heaven.

On the Iranian side, the drama was enacted between two poles, two co-eternal spirits. But although, before Manicheism the spirit-matter distinction was never identified with that between good and evil, in Zarathushtra is to be found the notion, analogous to the Platonic conception of the spirit-matter relationship, that the evil spirit is purely negative and destructive, a sheer limit to God's power.

Later on, this conception was to become coarser when Ahriman was conceived increasingly as the counterpart of Ormazd in the coarse and rigid dualism reflected notably in the Videvdat. This was probably the work of the Magians of Media. However, although Manicheism may have been the only Gnostic movement to adopt this extreme form of dualism, it may well, on the other hand, have been combined with the pessimistic, anti-cosmic tendency which subsisted on the fringe of Zoroastrianism, to give rise to Gnosticism.

The latter, with its asceticism that sometimes turned into ethical indifference, certainly seems to have derived from the meeting of Greek and Iranian elements, partly similar and partly complementary to each other, not excluding the Babylonian features and other Semitic elements. The meeting may even have taken place on Semitic ground, in Samaria, for instance, but probably independently in several places, for Gnosticism was a movement and not a sect.

Heretical Gnosticism, once it had become the powerful religion it developed into in the second and third centuries, was soon reflected in Iran. This came about, not only in Zervanism and Manicheism, but also in orthodox Mazdaism. We may recall in this respect the idea that the salvation of the world will be the work of successive saviours, all incarnations of one and the same primeval saviour. On the non-orthodox Christian side the Pseudo-Clementine Recognitions may be quoted, which teach that the saviour of men should be a man, and that he will be the very same man already incarnate in Adam, Enoch, etc.

The Gnostic tendency appears in cosmogony. According to at least two texts, when beings receive material form, Ormazd is moved to perform this creation in reply to Ahriman's attack. The initiative in material creation, therefore, belongs to the evil spirit.

The end of the world is sometimes conceived, not as the beginning of a new world, of happiness for the good and punishment or destruction for the wicked, but as a return of creation to God, or rather as a reabsorption into him of what had emanated from him.

In cosmology there is a remarkable and manifest compromise between the ancient Iranian religion which made gods of the heavenly bodies and Gnosticism or Manicheism which makes them demons. Official Mazdaism regarded only the planets as demons, the sun, moon and stars remaining gods.

Finally, when under Islam mysticism invaded Iran from east and west, it found there favourable ground after all. Had not Suhrawardi, who died in 491, felt himself to be at once the heir of Iran and Greece? Thanks to him, for the first and only time, the Mazdaean archangels espoused their sisters, the Ideas of Plato.

SELECT BIBLIOGRAPHY

(An asterisk denotes works by non-Catholics)

*ALBRIGHT, W. F.: *The Archeology of Palestine*, London and Baltimore, Pelican, 1949.

*BAILEY, H. W.: *Zoroastrian Problems in the Early Ninth Century Books*, Oxford and New York, Oxford Univ. Press, 1943.

*BELL, H. I.: *Cults and Creeds in Graeco-Roman Egypt*, Oxford and New York, Oxford Univ. Press, 1953.

*BREASTED, J. H.: *Development of Religion and Thought in Ancient Egypt*, London, Hodder and Stoughton, 1912.

*BURKITT, F. C.: *The Religion of the Manichees*, Cambridge and New York, Cambridge Univ. Press, 1925.

*CERNY, J.: *Ancient Egyptian Religion*, New York, Rinehart, 1952.

*DRIVER, G. R. and MILES, J. C.: *Babylonian Laws*, two volumes, Oxford and New York, Oxford Univ. Press, 1955–6.

DUCHESNE-GUILLEMIN, J.: *The Western Response to Zoroaster*, Oxford and New York, Oxford Univ. Press, 1959.

DUCHESNE-GUILLEMIN, J.: *Hymns of Zarathustra*, Hollywood-by-the-Sea, Fla, Transatlantic, 1954.

*FRANKFORT, H.: *Kingship and the Gods*, Chicago, University of Chicago, 1948.

*GURNEY, O. R.: *The Hittites*, London and Baltimore, Penguin, 1952.

*HOOKE, S. H.: *Babylonian and Assyrian Religion*, New York, Rinehart, 1953.

*JOHNS, C. H. W.: *The Oldest Code of Laws in the World, The Code of Laws promulgated by Hammurabi, King of Babylon, B.C. 2285–2242*, Edinburgh, Clark, 1903.

*McCOWN, C. C.: *The Ladder of Progress in Palestine*, New York, Harper, 1943.

*SMITH, Margaret: *Studies in Early Mysticism in the Near Middle East*, London, Sheldon Press, 1931.

VIERA, M.: *Hittite Art 2300–750 B.C.*, London, Tiranti, and Hollywood-by-the-Sea, Fla, Transatlantic, 1953.

ZAEHNER, R. C.: *Zurvan, a Zoroastrian Dilemma*, Oxford and New York, Oxford Univ. Press, 1955.

ZAEHNER, R. C.: *The Teachings of the Magi*, London, George Allen and Unwin and New York, Macmillan, 1956.

ABOUT THE AUTHOR

RENATA ADLER was born in Milan, Italy, and grew up mainly in Danbury, Connecticut. She attended Bryn Mawr College, where she majored in philosophy and German; the Sorbonne, where she received a D.d'É.S. in philosophy with Jean Wahl and Claude Levi-Strauss; and Harvard, where she is still a student in comparative literature. In 1962 she became a staff writer-reporter for *The New Yorker*. From January, 1968, to March, 1969, she was film critic of *The New York Times*.